The Plebeians Rehearse the Uprising

GÜNTER GRASS

The Plebeians Rehearse the Uprising

A German Tragedy

With an Introductory Address
by the Author

Translated by Ralph Manheim

A Helen and Kurt Wolff Book
Harcourt, Brace & World, Inc., New York

Library of Congress Catalog Card Number: 66–23810
Printed in the United States of America

ISBN 0-15-672050-7

D E F G H I J

Originally published in Germany under the title *Die Plebejer proben den Aufstand*

Contents

The Prehistory and Posthistory of the Tragedy of *Coriolanus* from Livy and Plutarch via Shakespeare down to Brecht and Myself

Address given at the Academy of Arts and Letters, Berlin, April 23, 1964, the quatercentenary of Shakespeare's birth

Let's assume that there was such a man—complete with goatee and earrings as in the Chandos portrait. Let's further assume that a quarrel with his wife or some trouble over poaching drove him from Stratford, and that he went to London, where, as the titles of the *Complete Works* would have us believe, he wrote more than thirty plays and pursued the career of an actor. If it amuses us, we can fancy him taking female roles: did he play the part of Goneril, or was he Cordelia? But this much is certain: the Globe Theater burned down on June 29, 1613, after his return to Stratford. Still, I should find it easier to regard him as an arsonist, a man who deliberately destroyed the evidence of his existence, than to honor Queen Elizabeth as the true author of his plays, especially as Sir Francis Bacon or the Earl of Southampton may have written them. It is amusing to speculate on half-way documented anecdotes and to conclude that his friend and rival Ben Jonson, who belabored him with advice at the Mermaid Tavern (for instance, that he should not accede to every whim, but should file and polish more and pay more attention to art), that Ben Jonson, who addressed him in a poem as "gentle Shakespeare," though refusing to take his word for it that Bohemia was situated on the seacoast, murdered him in 1616, in the course of a drinking bout. Be that as it may, we know for sure that in his last will and testament he bequeathed his second-best bed to his wife. We are not so sure that on April 23, 1564, he was born like common mortals and that he wrote twenty-seven or twenty-eight, or perhaps only twenty-one plays. He learned from Marlowe, Nashe, and Greene. He lifted plots and whole scenes from Holinshed, his bedside chronicler, from Plutarch, and from fellow playwrights, living and dead. He took material from Kyd and ideas from Montaigne. Falstaff and the puritan Malvolio are indeed his own brain children, but like all so-called original creations they were begotten by other fathers. For without Marlowe's *Jew of Malta* there would be no *Merchant of Venice*. It was a period of give and take. This practice was to become popular: all subject matter is free; let other owners fence in their property, the real estate of the mind is fair game for all. Bertolt Brecht had in common with William Shakespeare not only an aptitude for becoming a classic but also a deep-seated indifference to claims of literary ownership. Brecht once said to Kerr, the critic, who was rather a stickler in such matters: "Obviously the basis of just about every great age in literature is the force and innocence of its plagiarism."

But it is not easy to steal, and it is even harder to "adapt." There was lightness of touch in Brecht's borrowing from Marlowe and Lenz. But while he was transforming the tragedy of Coriolanus into the didactic play *Coriolan,* the god who protects all thieves of literary property was far away.

The preface to my edition of Shakespeare says: "Because of its antidemocratic character, the play is seldom produced." It is this antidemocratic bias and its reversal that I wish to discuss here—"The Prehistory and Posthistory of the Tragedy of Coriolanus from Livy and Plutarch via Shakespeare down to Brecht and Myself." Presumption has the floor!

When Shakespeare was nineteen years old, an English

translation of Plutarch appeared in London He took the plot of his *Coriolanus* from Plutarch's life of the Roman hero. It is safe to say that he did not read the Greek original, because the English translator's mistakes came to roost in his play. A few years later he moved to London and his Plutarch went with him.

The bare plot is as follows: The plebeians of Rome are about to rise against the patricians. Their grievances are the price of grain and Caius Marcius—the future Coriolanus. A war breaks out with the nearby Volscians. To induce the plebeians to join the army, the patricians agree to the appointment of tribunes, empowered to defend the cause of the people before the Senate. In the course of the war, the plebeians prove to be cowards intent on loot, while Caius Marcius, the enemy of the people, shows himself to be a noble hero, who declines any share in the spoils. Thanks to his intrepid courage, the Romans take the city of Corioli, after which he is surnamed Coriolanus. On his return to Rome, he is applauded by the formerly hostile plebeians. Though he continues to mock and revile them, they even wish to elect him consul; but his election is blocked by the intrigues of the tribunes and by his own mounting arrogance. The old antagonism between plebeians and patricians revives. Coriolanus' vituperation provokes violence. The patricians are no longer able to defend him. Banished by the people, he leaves Rome and goes over to the enemy. The Volscians welcome him, their victorious enemy, as an ally against hated Rome: at the head of the Volscian army he threatens his native city. When none of his patrician friends can persuade him to turn back, his mother goes out to the Volscian camp. Her words have the desired effect. Because his mother has dissuaded him from betraying his native city, he becomes a traitor to his allies: he is murdered, but his murderers, the Volscian commanders, respect his greatness and honor his memory.

In the Coriolanus legend events that took place at the end of the Roman kingdom and others which occurred down to the end of the Gallic Wars are lumped together as if they had all taken place somewhere around 500 B.C., and as if the installation of tribunes of the people, which Livy describes as a gradual development, had occurred from one day to the next. According to Mommsen, the legend sprang from the desire of two plebeian families to prove their antiquity. According to Livy, the wife and mother of Coriolanus came of these families, the Volumni and the Veturi. Shakespeare gives no inkling of this; his play mentions no ties of kinship between the contending forces: the ancient nobility and the faceless plebeians.

Tersely puncturing any attempt to harness this tragedy to partisan aims, Heine wrote: "Sometimes one inclines to think that Shakespeare is a modern poet, living in present-day London and aiming to portray the present-day Tories and Whigs in Roman masks."

This play is fated to be looked upon at all times as a reflection of modern conditions, for at the time when it was written, contending parties confronted one another on the streets of London in very much the same way as the patricians and plebeians, the Tories and the Whigs. Innovators, sectarians, and rebels made the island acquainted with the world, for in England the destruction of the Spanish Armada ushered in the seventeenth century. The East India Company was founded; expeditions marked out the spheres of future English power. While Shakespeare's contemporary Cervantes was creating the "knight of the mournful countenance" out of his own defeats and those of Spain, the Elizabethan theater was putting colossal conquerors on the stage, from Marlowe's *Tamburlaine* to Shakespeare's *Coriolanus*.

Between 1605 and 1608, in the four years during which Shakespeare conceived and wrote his tragedy, a number of political events gave him first-hand knowledge of what we today call the class struggle: in 1607 the peasants revolted because of the confiscation by the nobles of communally held lands; in 1604 the Gunpowder Plot was discovered: papists had tried to blow up the predominantly Puritan Parliament; in 1606, the plague began once again to assume serious proportions in London, and it seems likely that all the theaters were closed while Shakespeare was writing *Coriolanus*.

Plays, books, even poems, which timid souls today like to call "timeless," were being written by men who, even if ancient Rome provided the backdrop, were looking out the window at their own times and listening to what was going on in the streets. Coriolanus' uncouthness, to be sure, comes from Plutarch, who attributed it to his fatherless upbringing, but it was Shakespeare's London that provided the coarse, lewd idiom, the rich vocabulary of vilification he puts into the mouths of Coriolanus, of the patrician Menenius, and of Volumnia, the hero's mother; and indeed, the character of Coriolanus is largely portrayed through the crude outpourings, rising in intensity from scene to scene, of his monstrous arrogance. And once we conclude, with good reason, that Shakespeare had a living model for this portrait, we come upon the obvious, if undocumented, theory which assigns that role to Sir Walter Raleigh, the imperious pirate, a knighted and distinguished patriot. For the fate of Raleigh, a friend of Ben Jonson (so why not of Shakespeare?), was not unlike that of Coriolanus: After he had captured a silver fleet from the Spaniards, fought for the Queen of England in Cádiz and the Azores, and conquered vast regions in America—as Coriolanus had conquered his Corioli—he was almost killed by the mob in 1604, while being arrested on the order of King James I. Formerly idolized, Raleigh had made himself unpopular, while to the victorious Coriolanus the plebeians had given their votes only to retract them shortly afterward. In the tragedy, as in London, we hear of the hero's contempt for the poor. Raleigh controlled the wine monopoly; Coriolanus controlled all the grain ships coming from Sicily. While in Rome the enemy of the people prevented captured grain stores from being distributed among the indigent, in London the naval hero bitterly opposed a bill before Parliament which provided for the sale of cheap wine. Both heroes forfeited the favor of the people when, no longer contenting themselves with their trades of war and piracy, they carried the ways of the warlord and pirate into commerce and tried, the one in the grain, the other in the wine market, to fix prices, that is, to keep them high.

This is not to say that *Coriolanus* is an outright drama à clef, but there is no doubt that the period when the Puritans were on the rise and the recently knighted soldiers of fortune on the wane finds its reflection in the play. When for the one hundredth time the Puritans tried to shut down the Globe Theater as a breeding place of sin and pestilence, the insults which Burbage, its director, heaped on the fanatical petits bourgeois may well have been as colorful as those with which in Rome, according to Shakespeare, the plebeians demanded modesty and democratic bearing of Coriolanus. Even if the reactionary—from a historical point of view—character of *Coriolanus* has paled with time, it was then glaringly obvious and stood in the way of the play's performance; for—and not least in the interest of his theater—the author warns the king and nobles of the rise of the artisans and the common people, that is, of the Puritans and of Parliament, three quarters of whose members were Puritans. History has spoken twice against Shakespeare's play: Livy tells us that thirty-six years after the election of the first tribunes, their number was increased to ten: the People's Tribunate, Rome's greatest achievement, an achievement valid to this day, had prevailed. And in England, forty years after the completion of *Coriolanus,* Cromwell, the Lord Protector, was at the helm. Shakespeare's theater was closed even earlier. What has remained, along with a good deal more, is this bothersome play, in which Rome's plebeians, like London's artisans, are cowardly rats and ignorant dogs, in which Roman patricians, like English nobles, are noble lords and heroes without taint.

These antagonisms and the cold light in which they are displayed have to this day barred *Coriolanus* from the stage. True, the play is not lacking in poetry—"Anger's my meat . . ." says Volumnia—but this poetry strides along in frosty passion. It feeds on arrogance, presumption, injured pride, intrigue born of hate, and time and again on quickly mounting anger. There is no room for tenderness, for Shakespeare puts no lovers, not even mild madness in the shape of woman or fool, in the path of the inevitable action. No ghosts or sprites, no meeting of witches, no fantastic exposition—as in *King Lear*—allow the language to soar above the earthly. On earth there is no possibility other than standing or brawling. The heavens are impenetrable. The gods are far away and take no part. And even the colossal figure of Coriolanus, he who has the stuff for a god of war, is not permitted to stand dispassionately aside, building up the momentum for a soaring soliloquy. He is always hemmed in by plebeians or their tribunes, by supporters or enemies, and, in his most solitary movements, by his family; for when his arrogance rises to a blasphemous pitch which, if no one disturbed him, might develop into a monologue, he is immediately interrupted by a tribune, or his friend Menenius tries to appease him: "Come, come, you have been too rough, something too rough."

It is not the all too familiar ambiguity of the hero that has stood in the way of this play from the first; rather it is his brutal outrightness that sets him between plebeian and patrician and prevents him from arousing the faintest sympathy or applause in either a proletarian or a conservative audience. What even a monster like Richard III succeeds in making us believe—namely, that his daemon drives him to give us the shudders and so entertain us—the earthly and unintellectual Coriolanus fails to accomplish in a single scene. And even his few virtues, such as his modesty, his unwillingness to show the plebeians his wounds and scars, his selfless bravery, are obscured by his compulsion, whenever he encounters a plebeian, to proclaim his truth: scorn, contempt, and hatred. Richard can be led by guile to slip into contrasting roles: Coriolanus is a hero who can only be as he is and not otherwise. The patrician Menenius and Coriolanus' mother Volumnia persuade him, against his better judgment, to be crafty, to proceed with diplomacy. But in the presence of the detested plebeians, his efforts to be gracious turn, after the first exchange of words with the tribunes, into new provocations. Only once, when he has all the power in his hands and stands at the walls of Rome with the Volscian army, does he relent and then, quite consistently with the logic of the situation, he comes to grief. Volumnia and the two other women confront the unyielding colossus as a monumental group. Volumnia's words move him more than they convince him: this man, almost a god of war, becomes an obedient son, who spares his native city, allowing his hatred and lust for vengeance to seep away; he acts in opposition to his nature and is lost; for even in his downfall Coriolanus is irretrievably what he is. Though he gives in to his mother, he plays out his part incorrigibly to the end, and no party can claim him for itself by putting a new interpretation on him, because he is not the least bit ambiguous, and in addition, because the other characters of the play, patricians, plebeians, and Volscians, cluster around him, mirroring and multiplying his unambiguousness. For this reason I wish here to show, on the basis of the *Coriolan* adaptation, why Brecht's attempt to salvage this play for himself and his Berliner Ensemble was doomed to failure. As for Jan Kott, his attempt to interpret this as a modern play on the ground that its indigestibility makes it modern—to call its fate class struggle—puts him historically in the right if we lean more toward Livy than toward Plutarch. But it is a misinterpretation of Shakespeare the Elizabethan, who even strips Plutarch, his source, of his last whiff of class struggle: much as he numbers himself among the patricians, Coriolanus stands between the two classes; tribunes and consuls are more likely to get together—and later they do—than is the colossal exception to come to terms with the senate.

I have never been privileged to see Shakespeare's *Coriolanus* on the stage; and I am almost willing to make a bet with any and all of our distinguished producers that none of our subsidized theaters will find either the time or the appetite, during this Shakespeare year, to include this forever green, hence sour apple in its program. Only in the fief of our second Shakespeare Society, in the Theater am Schiffbauerdamm,[1] has the play gone into rehearsal, and I am curious to find out whether the Berliner Ensemble will select Brecht's unfinished adaptation, Lenz's Storm-and-Stress translation, the traditional Shakespeare text translated by Dorothea Tieck, or a conglomeration of all three. But regardless of which toboggan slide they choose to risk, the crucial question remains: What is your attitude toward the tribunes of the people? How are you going to handle Act I, Scene 1, the uprising of the plebeians? And once the switches are set: Does the play end as a tragedy with obligatory funeral march after the murder of a giant named Coriolanus; or, in accordance with Brecht's wishes, do the tribunes have the last word in a didactic play? For in Shakespeare these tribunes are pusillanimous rebels from the first; in Brecht they are re-educated, not in the course of the action but before they so much as appear on the stage, into staunch revolutionaries, who in the final scene are expected to prove that—as Livy intimates—the class-conscious plebeians are assured of victory. His tribunes behave in accordance with this thesis: while Shakespeare displays two interchangeable zeros, both cowardly schemers, Brecht gradually transfers the power to two shrewd and progressive functionaries. While Shakespeare makes his Coriolanus a man of the highest merit, whose tragic end is brought about by slight failings, pride swelling to arrogance and a sense of class verging on priggishness, Brecht reduces his Coriolan to the level of an efficient specialist, who, though useful in time of war, oversteps his functions in peacetime and is therefore dismissed by the people and its elected tribunes. Shakespeare's hero comes to grief first over his own passion and then, outwardly, over the pettiness of the plebeians; Brecht's Coriolan is swept aside because he behaves like a reactionary

[1] East Berlin Theater, of which Bertolt Brecht was the director.

and fails to understand the signs of the times, the springtime of the young Roman Republic. Shakespeare did everything in his power to bring out the dark, tragic greatness of his hero, quite consistently portraying the plebeians as tawdry petits bourgeois and the two tribunes as mediocre schemers, and even stripping the patrician Menenius Agrippa of his aura, attested both in Livy and in Plutarch, as a sage and friend of the plebeians, to make him a comic slyboots à la Polonius. Brecht's self-appointed task, from the very start, was to endow the plebeians with class consciousness and the tribunes with persuasive power. But where were these qualities to be found when not only the original, but even the historical sources and the reality outside his own windows, refused to provide them? Indeed, if a single tribune had been an antagonist comparable in weight to Coriolanus—and Plutarch tells us that one of them, Sicinius, was the "more energetic" —the play might have been titled "Sicinius and Coriolanus"; but even in Shakespeare's day word had got around that officials like best to operate in pairs and to state their business two-by-two and interchangeably. Actually the Senate had granted the plebeians five tribunes, and Shakespeare too speaks in passing of five: Coriolanus, however, can remember only the names of two:

> "One's Junius Brutus,
> Sicinius Velutus, and I know not—'Sdeath!"

In Brecht the reference to five elected tribunes is lacking, he merely gives an intimation of the plural:

> "Two tribunes
> To put forth their mob wisdom.
> The one is Junius Brutus, then there's
> Sicinius, and the Lord knows . . ."

His Coriolan warns:

> "Now they'll become
> More insolent than ever, threatening revolution
> Over every pound of olives."

While Shakespeare has him say:

"... it will in time
Win greater power and throw forth greater themes
For insurrection's arguing."

Let us dwell a moment on Brecht's olives, the cheapest of the articles demanded by the plebeians, a pound of which might suffice to stir the mob to rebellion. While Shakespeare, following Plutarch, attributed the unrest and the popular demands to the excessive price of grain and the usurious rates of interest, and puts the emphasis on grain and interest, Brecht's Coriolan minimizes the demand for cheap grain, which in the original still sounds defensible, by making the plebeian demands generally ridiculous with the reference to mere olives. Coriolanus fears the rabble will gain still more and demand greater things; Coriolan flies into a rage at the thought that in the future every trifle may lead to disorder. In other words, he does not understand the tribunitian power, regards its representatives as mere nuisances, and, on their very first appearance, refers to them as:

"... faces
As though cut from the gallows."

In Shakespeare the hero's cold pride is not yet vented at this point. He ignores the tribunes and greets only the senators, who enter at the same time, with the formula of respect, "our best elders," which Brecht puts into the mouth of Menenius, whereupon he makes his Coriolan scoff:

"And there come
Their fresh-baked inspectors too."

In the following scene, after the war on the Volscians has been decided on, Coriolanus in both versions calls on the plebeians, in Shakespeare as "worshipful mutineers," in Brecht as "dear friends and troublemakers," to follow him to the war. The Volscians, he declares scornfully, have plenty of corn, the "rats" will be able to fill their bellies full. But while, in the original, Coriolanus and the senators go out and the citizens, according to the stage direction, steal away, in Brecht "all with the exception of the tribunes and citizens" go out, for the adapter has instructed his plebeians not to take Coriolanus at his word, because to do so would be to discredit the newly elected tribunes. Only after the tribune Brutus has bidden them enroll in the army and fight bravely for a better Rome—the theory of the just war—and after Brutus has promised the plebeians to fight during their absence "For corn, olives, and a remission of rent and interest . . ." are they permitted to leave the stage. From now on the scene looks the same in both versions: the tribunes remain behind, but they do not speak the same lines. In Shakespeare two benighted fools stand around, outdoing one another in weighing Coriolanus' courage against his arrogance, in listing his good and bad deeds. At the same time the author employs them in the service of poetry. Sicinius says that Coriolanus will "Bemock the modest moon."

In Brecht two self-reliant officials state their positions. Tersely and without recourse to moon-metaphors, Sicinius observes that this man is a greater danger to Rome than to the Volscians. But Brutus, recognizing that a military specialist can play an important role in a specific situation and confident in the success of his own cause, disagrees:

> "I do not think so. The sword of such a man
> Can do more good than his vices injury."

Whereupon both go out: in Brecht, self-confident toward an unnamed destination; in Shakespeare, stripped of their function, they head for the forum, in the hope of hearing something that will provide fuel for a possible intrigue.

In the original as in the adaptation, one of Coriolanus' strong points is his enormous gift for slinging strong and sometimes poetic words of vilification. It would be interesting to draw up a catalogue comparing Shakespeare's terms and Brecht's innovations, and beside it a list of contemporary political insults such as "cold-war warrior," "objectivist," "appeaser" and "ultra"; in connection with words of vilification, space permits us here to indicate at most how Brecht has sometimes watered down the original text, while sometimes, in line with the ax he is trying to grind, he has pointed it up.

A standing expletive of Coriolanus, whenever he runs across plebeians, is "Hang 'em!" Once, however, in the middle of a shattering tirade on the mean-spirited plebeians who carp at all greatness, he does not conclude with his usual "Hang 'em!" but, outdoing himself, suggests that they hang themselves ("Hang ye!"). Brecht was unable to take over this supreme insult, because it would indeed have turned his plebeians into worms. Instead he writes "Only hanging can help," without an exclamation mark—words which, for all their hostility, may be interpreted as the resigned sigh of a rough military man, who would like to restore order in the quickest way by stringing people up, but is not permitted to employ this direct method.

In the battle scenes of the Volscian war, a single example may suffice to show how Shakespeare went about tapping a source. Corioli has already been taken. The spoils are to be distributed. Plutarch relates how a tenth part of the booty and a caparisoned horse are offered to Marcius, who has captured the city. But our hero is not interested in material gains and after the Romans have applauded him for his magnanimity, expresses one desire: " 'I have only,' said he, 'one special grace to beg, and this I hope you will not deny me. There was a certain hospitable friend of mine among the Volscians, a man of probity and virtue, who is become a prisoner, and from former wealth and freedom is now reduced to servitude. Among his many misfortunes let my intercession redeem him from the one of being sold as a common slave.' "—In Plutarch then, the host's name is not stated, but we may reasonably expect him to be saved. What dramatic bite Shakespeare draws from this idyll of magnanimity!

Caius Marcius, just honored with the name of Coriolanus, presents his request:

"I sometime lay here in Corioli
At a poor man's house; he us'd me kindly.
He cried to me; I saw him prisoner;
But then Aufidius was within my view,
And wrath o'erwhelmed my pity. I request you
To give my poor host freedom."

Cominius, the general, replies:

"O, well begg'd!
Were he the butcher of my son, he should
Be free as the wind. Deliver him, Titus."

And now Titus asks to know what Plutarch also fails to mention:

"Marcius, his name?"

And Coriolanus, as I see it, slaps his forehead:

"By Jupiter, forgot!
I am weary; yea, my memory is tir'd.
Have we no wine here?"

He obtains the wine forthwith on Cominius' order, and his wounds are bound; but we never hear another word about the nameless host who is supposed to be set free.

Brecht never completed the battle scenes, four to ten, which he intended to telescope into a single Scene 3; otherwise it would be illuminating to find out whether he deleted the poor Volscian, or which one he helped, Plutarch's or Shakespeare's doubly unfortunate Volscian.

But let us stick to the available texts. Act II, Scene 1, when we compare the two versions, confirms Brecht's intention of transforming the original—even at the cost of sacrificing the most flowery passages of the dialogue—into a play of partisanship, in which Coriolan becomes an increasingly crude military specialist, the wise fool Menenius turns into a reactionary clown, and the two tribunes of the people are metamorphosed into class strugglers of the second if not the first water.

While the Menenius of the original disposes of the tribunes as two senile fools, ". . . ambitious for poor knaves' caps and legs," the Menenius of the adaptation suspects them of being far more dangerous. He sees them "as a couple of conceited, violent knaves without a country. . . ." And this last epithet, surely chosen by design, becomes a posterlike abridgment of Act II, Scene 1. For at this point Shakespeare parades another piece of elaborate exposition. The news of the victory at Corioli which, fortunate as it is for Rome, is bound to come as a terrible blow to the tribunes, is concealed by the cantankerous dialogue of three old men, one of whom, Menenius, after describing himself as "a humorous patrician, and one that loves a cup of hot wine," declares that the tribunes' only way of settling a dispute is to call both parties scoundrels. In describing the behavior of the two tribunes in court, in endowing them with a colic running parallel to the judicial proceedings, and making them roar for a chamber-pot, Shakespeare makes it clear that he has represented England's Puritan justices of the peace as Roman tribunes of the people, and a recently knighted London wag and drunkard as a patrician.

In Brecht little remains of this, probably too little. Heedless of impoverishing the text, he sticks to the essential, the skeleton of the exposition, and allows his tribunes to discuss coolly and objectively the advantages and disadvantages of the victory at Corioli. The dialogue with Menenius is reduced to a trifling though virulent squabble. Not he, but the tribunes dominate the scene.

As an example of how willful partisanship flattens out the details and tolerates poetry at most as an incidental ornament, I quote the following dialogue.

Menenius asks in the original:

"Pray you, who does the wolf love?"

The tribune Sicinius replies:

"The lamb."

Menenius completes the thought:

"Aye, to devour him, as the hungry plebeians would the noble Marcius."

Here Brutus, the other tribune, says:

"He's a lamb indeed, that baas like a bear."

Brecht does not allow his Brutus this bit of whimsy:

"He's a lamb indeed, that roars like a bear."

The humor of the bleating bear gives way to a solemn reminder of what a dangerous man this Marcius Coriolanus is: a roaring bear, pure and simple, and never a bear that can occasionally baa like a sheep.

Brecht showed us with his *Life of Edward II of England*, after Marlowe, how a powerful adaptation can breathe life into a play that has gone flat, how indeed it can give the original back to the stage. He did not succeed in doing the same for *Coriolanus*. His version has deprived the tragedy of its naïve plot and replaced it with a hard-working mechanism, which does its stint and makes its partisanship sound pleasantly aesthetic; but since I am here trying to justify "the theft of literary property" as practiced by the Elizabethan theater and by the early Brecht, it seems worthwhile to go on showing that where the spoils are so meager as in the present case literary piracy does not pay.

In the following scene—Volumnia, Virgilia, and Valeria meet Menenius—Brecht has his tribunes leave before the group occupies the stage, and for no apparent reason throws out one of the most delightfully absurd pieces of dialogue, the discussion of Coriolanus' wounds, which foreshadows the entrance of the hero and gives an intimation of his gigantic dimensions. In Shakespeare, Menenius asks in the presence of the shamed tribune:

> "Where is he wounded?"

Volumnia, the mother, answers:

> "I' th' shoulder and i' th' left arm; there will be large cicatrices to show the people when he shall stand for his place. He received in the repulse of Tarquin seven hurts i' th' body."

Menenius knows exactly where:

> "One i' th' neck and two i' th' thigh—there's nine that I know."

Volumnia goes the old man one better:

> "He had, before this last expedition, twenty-five wounds upon him."

Menenius figures:

> "Now it's twenty-seven; every gash was an enemy's grave."

Trumpets and martial shouts announce the arrival of Marcius Coriolanus. Twenty-seven salvoes would not have prepared his entrance as well as so many wounds counted up on fingers. Brecht forgoes this wealth of scars. After an abbreviated dialogue he contents himself with nine. In so doing he destroys the motive of the preparatory dialogue, for in his version an old soldier will have to run for consul with a plausible number of scars. When Shakespeare's walking arsenal of scars is shamed to exhibit his marks to garner votes, we sympathize with him; to Brecht such sympathy was inadmissible.

But let us have the tribunes step forward again. Coriolanus has gone to the Capitol with his retinue. While in the original the old men began to spin their intrigue, the representatives of the people in the adaptation prove to be loyal patriots, who would frown on intrigue as an instrument of struggle. Colorfully and at length, Shakespeare's Brutus deplores the behavior of London's rabble in the streets of Rome; in Brecht all that remains of this is a brief statement of Sicinius:

> "What a fuss,
> As though a god had descended on the world!
> He will be consul, believe me, in a twinkling."

The adapter even throws out the spectacles of the plebeians—an anachronistic gift of Shakespeare to the Romans—but since Sicinius' speech is now utterly colorless, he puts in a little color of his own:

> "And listen, how a Rome grown drunk on victory
> Echoes with the victory of the insubordinate
> man. . . ."

Brecht's tribunes call Coriolanus "insubordinate" because they believe he has overstepped his authority. Sicinius says: "His mission was to repel the Volscians—no more." They find fault with him for needlessly capturing and devastating the city of Corioli. Brutus fears he has stirred up the Volscians against the people of Rome for many years to come. Shakespeare's tribunes are incapable of such concern for their country. They are delighted that their neighbors have not only received a drubbing but lost several strongpoints and a large part of their territory as well. To their minds Coriolanus' overweening oppression of the people is reason enough for them to cook up an intrigue that will encompass his downfall. Brecht does not eliminate this theme, but he soft-pedals it by treating Coriolanus' arrogance more briefly, putting more calculation into his unthinking rage, and transforming the vulgar despiser of the common people into a conscious enemy of the people. In addition, Brecht introduces an argument lacking in Shakespeare: while Brecht's tribunes act strictly in accord with constitutional democracy, Coriolanus' sole role is that of the soldier who usurps rights at every step. Here the adaptation is based on Livy. Brecht's aim is to extract a lesson, both for himself and for his audience, from early Roman history. He points to the established position of the tribunes and of the aediles assigned to them. Accordingly, the illegality of Coriolanus' acts is far more blatant in the adaptation than in the original, which represents Coriolanus' failure as neither right nor wrong but the work of blind fate; the hero's growing pride, the intrigue of the tribunes, and his mother's words that constrain him to turn back, are merely the tripwires that provide the tragedy with its catastrophe.

Rome. Senate. Capitol. Tribunes and aediles. Latin names. Material taken from Plutarch. And nevertheless the question must be asked: Is *The Tragedy of Coriolanus* a historical play, or is Rome merely a convenient setting, where we learn more about the decline of the Elizabethan period than about the development of Rome from a monarchy to a constitutional republic? Shakespeare's Rome cannot stand up under historical investigation and should not be measured by such a yardstick. The author had no Livy to advise him, and as for his chronicler, Plutarch, who to the catalogue of Roman virtues adds the lessons of his own late Greek education, Shakespeare bends him to his own purposes, drops him half despoiled, and a while later snatches him up again, as if by whim, to ransack him some more. He mixes the spoils with the loot from other raids, eliminates the Greek's pedagogical warmth, and replaces it with fate and inexorable nature. While Plutarch explains the decline and downfall of his hero by saying that he had lacked a father and a father's guiding hand, in Shakespeare the whole play is pervaded by a smoldering mother complex that leaves no room for any attempt at education. He wins victories, collects wounds, partly for his country no doubt, but primarily in order to lay the conquered city at his mother's feet, in order to enrich his mother's collection of scars; for she, Volumnia, treats her son like a lover, while his squeamish wife Virgilia, who can neither bear the sight of blood nor look upon the hero's scars as wealth, must content herself with the role of mother to the little

Marcius, who, however, as the hero's son, lives entirely in the aura of the hero's mother and, though still scarless, takes after his father. Volumnia says:

> "He had rather see the swords and hear a drum than look upon his schoolmaster."

Whereupon Valeria, the friend of the family, tells how very much and how delightfully he resembles his father:

> "I saw him run after a gilded butterfly; and when he caught it he let it go again, and after it again, and over and over he comes, and up again, catch'd it again; or whether his fall enrag'd him, or how 'twas, he did so set his teeth and tear it."

To which the hero's mother replies:

> "One on 's father's moods."

And Valeria ironically:

> "Indeed, la, 'tis a noble child."

But the gentle Virgilia remarks:

> "A crack" [a little rascal].

Here as in other plays Shakespeare duplicates his hero. In the child he underlines the father's traits, but withholds comment except for Valeria's irony, and lets the mangling of the butterfly speak for itself. Brecht, however, does not forgo commentary. In his version the comments of Volumnia and Virgilia are sharpened and become words of reproach.

"One on 's father's moods" becomes "One of his father's fits of rage!" And Virgilia's "A crack" is not addressed to her friend Valeria. Transformed into "A little brute," it becomes a challenge flung at her mother-in-law.

Plutarch's pedagogic motivation thus finds an echo in the Brecht adaptation: Shakespeare's intention to enlarge his hero's barbaric stature by duplicating him is in Brecht transformed into a didactic intention: the father's excesses receive their confirmation in the son as, at the same time, the latent conflict emerges between daughter-in-law and mother-in-law.

But after so thorough a study of the sources, did Brecht, any more than Shakespeare, set out to create a historical play? With his text based on Plutarch's pedagogy and Livy's republican feeling for constitutional government, does he give a more accurate picture of Rome after the banishment of King Tarquin? Brecht takes this path hesitantly and abandons it without a qualm as soon as his self-imposed thesis demands it. Moreover, the Elizabethan figure of Coriolanus, nourished by Raleigh and Essex, is unable to develop in the broad epic material of Livy's history, to which Brecht gives little dramatic condensation. Brecht, it is true, can invoke Livy's authority when he reduces the colossal fate-driven figure to a military specialist, for Roman history shows how quickly and easily General Caius Marcius, surnamed Coriolanus, was replaced, but Shakespeare put words into the mouth of his hero that a military specialist would not even be able to read from the written page. This probably explains why Brecht intellectualized his Coriolan, for otherwise he would have lost too much in adapting the original text. While Shakespeare, in the argument about the stored-up grain, refers only in passing to the fact that in Greece grain was sometimes distributed gratis to the people, Brecht exploits the Greek Plutarch and develops the dialogue between the tribunes and Coriolanus into a political debate.

Coriolan:

> "Whoever suggested giving out the corn
> From the storehouse gratis, as is perhaps
> Customary in Greece . . ."

The tribune Brutus interrupts him:

> "Wherever
> The people are really consulted, and not only on
> paper!"

To which Brecht's Coriolan has a solution which nowadays might have occurred to our Franz-Josef Strauss:

> "In Greece! Why then don't you go
> To Greece? This city is called Rome."

The adapter is still more inconclusive, vacillating between partisanship and history, in his treatment of Menenius Agrippa. Neither Livy nor Plutarch can save this sly old fool, because the source of his wit is neither Roman history nor late Greek moralizing, but plague-ridden and Puritan-ridden London. In Livy he is described as a wise and kindly patrician, whom the plebeians respect. Even before the conflict between the plebeians and Coriolanus he is elected consul. He is credited with a victory over the Aurunci. And when the plebeians, incited by a certain Sicinius, leave Rome and pitch camp on the sacred mountain near the city, it is Menenius Agrippa who persuades them to return home with the story of the parts of the body that rebel against the belly. In Livy the story goes: "Negotiations began and an agreement was reached on the condition that special magistrates should be appointed to represent the commons." Only then, provided with tribunes, are the plebeians willing to take up arms against the Volscians. In the course of the war young Marcius covers himself with glory. According to Livy, however, Menenius, who in Shakespeare's play stands by Coriolanus to the end of the tragedy, dies before anything tragic happens.

But the patrician beloved of the people ". . . did not leave enough wealth to provide for his burial. The citizens paid for his funeral, and each one," so says Livy, "contributed his bit."

In Plutarch, as well, Menenius Agrippa is mentioned only in connection with the parable of the belly and the rebellious parts of the body. Shakespeare, however, allows him neither to die nor to step aside after the first scenes. He needed the old gentleman as the companion and comic mirror of his hero; neither did Brecht want to do without him. In fact, the adaptation departs even further than the original from the historical source: while the London Menenius, thanks to his wit, meets with at least some sympathy among the plebeians, all contact is lost between the plebeians and a Menenius transformed into a feeble-minded reactionary.

Brecht's intention of using Plutarch's pedagogy and Livy's constitutionalism as props for his own teaching comes out most clearly in the new version of Volumnia. Both sources represent her, the hero's mother, as a virtuous Roman matron, to whom custom, law, and country mean more than her erring son. Shakespeare raised this stern woman to the same heroic dimensions as her son. Furthermore, she fills in the blanks in his character, she has the guile, the diplomacy, he lacks, and knows how to lie when the situation calls for it. Even when she makes him turn back and spare his native city, she tries to build a diplomatic bridge for him. She advises him to bring about peace between the Volscians and the Romans: thus he will go down in history not as a traitor to both causes but as the great peacemaker. Apart from this, Plutarch's moralizing is cast aside as soon as Shakespeare takes Volumnia in hand. Her curses and blasphemies—

> "Now the red pestilence strike all trades in Rome,
> And occupations perish!"—

are as consummate as her son's vilification of the plebeians. But though she is Coriolanus' equal, the law of this tragedy places her in the chorus of the tribunes and plebeians, patricians and Volscians, of all those who either work toward, or are unable to prevent, Coriolanus' downfall. The guile and deceit she recommends to her son are her contribution to his doom. By compelling this incorrigible man to dissemble, she makes him muddle his autocratic role:

> "Like a dull actor now
> I have forgot my part and I am out. . . ."

He has shaken off Volscians and plebeians; the tribunes were to him a laughingstock; but her monologue—and only to Volumnia is this weapon granted—shatters his designs and breaks him. Only a moment before, as he saw the women approaching, he admonished himself:

"I'll never
Be such a gosling to obey instinct, but stand
As if a man were author of himself
And knew no other kin."

But now that Volumnia has spoken, he clasps her hands:

"O my mother, mother! O!
You have won a happy victory to Rome;
But for your son—believe it, O, believe it!—
Most dangerously you have with him prevailed,
If not most mortal to him. But let it come."

In Brecht we have a different Volumnia. It is not by her own decision alone, as in the original, that she appears before the walls of the city; she has come to the Volscian camp at the behest of the patricians and no less of the tribunes. While Shakespeare's Volumnia wishes to move her son and to save him with her final suggestion that he proceed with diplomacy, I can hear Helene Weigel pronouncing the adapted text and condemning her son:

"Enough of childish mawkishness, know
That you are marching on a very different Rome
From the one you left. You are no longer
Indispensable; you're nothing but
A mortal peril for all. Wait not for the smoke
Of submission! If you see smoke now
It will arise from smithies forging
Swords against you. . . ."

Having written off her son, she brusquely leaves the stage with the other women. Even in Plutarch there is no such strait-laced coldness. Shakespeare follows him in allowing his hero to drink a last cup of kindness with the ladies.

In the next scene of the adaptation, the upgrading of the tribunes who have used Volumnia as a mouthpiece is shown even more blatantly. In the original, while the patrician Menenius and the tribune Sicinius are expressing their anxiety about the outcome of the women's mission, a messenger comes and advises the terrified Sicinius to flee: the people have seized Brutus, his fellow tribune, they are dragging him through the streets and are threatening to put him to death "by inches" if the women bring no good news. Only then does a second messenger arrive to announce the withdrawal of the Volscians under Coriolanus. In Brecht all that remains of this tense scene, once again revealing the cowardice of the tribunes, is two terse phrases which serve partisanship, and nothing else. The messenger appears:

> "News!
> The Volscians are withdrawing and Marcius with
> them!"

The tribune Brutus, whom here the people have no desire to drag through the streets, who, in place of the now functionless patrician Menenius, is standing with Sicinius, says:

> "The stone has moved. The people are in arms,
> And the old earth trembles."

The last scene of the original and the next to last in the adaptation show the murder of Coriolanus by the Volscians in a public place in Antium. In the original the murder comes as the culmination of an old and in no small part private feud between two patricians: Aufidius and Coriolanus have always fought one another as social equals; and when Coriolanus, after being banished from Rome by the plebeians, becomes the ally of his former enemy, this personal conflict between two nobles plays an important role. In the end, accordingly, the Volscian lords praise Coriolanus as noble and laden with glory. No sooner have Aufidius and the conspirators struck him down than he is mourned. Aufidius speaks the final words in honor of Coriolanus:

> "My rage is gone,
> And I am struck with sorrow . . ."

Coriolanus' body is carried away. A funeral march is the only music in this tragedy.

In Brecht someone who is superfluous and whose role has long since been played out is coldly and mechanically put out of the way. No funeral march. No honor to his memory. And the play has still another scene to offer, in which the tribunes say the last word. Rome. The Senate. Consuls, senators, and tribunes are assembled in session. A law is passed, a motion raised. A messenger brings the news of the murder of Caius Marcius, formerly Coriolanus. Menenius makes a motion that the name of the once great, later unfortunate hero be immortalized in the Capitol. Brutus sweeps the motion from the table:

> "I move
> That the Senate proceed with current business."

A nameless consul plucks up the courage to speak:

> "A question:
> The Marcians ask that in accordance with
> Numa Pompilius' decree concerning
> Surviving kin of fathers, sons, and brothers,
> Their womenfolk be given permission to wear
> Mourning in public for ten moons."

Plutarch relates that this request was granted; Livy confirms neither the death of Coriolanus nor a period of mourning, but cites Fabius as recording that Coriolanus had lived to a ripe old age; Brecht here forsakes Shakespeare, Plutarch, and his special source, Livy. With no other foundation than himself and the intent underlying his adaptation, he makes the tribune Brutus censure the motion for a period of mourning with one final word: "Rejected."

There exists a strange tetralogue entitled: "A study of the first scene of Shakespeare's *Coriolanus*." In it Brecht tried to record his preliminary discussions with his assistants. In places the result has an involuntary humor, because—though cast in four parts—it is always Brecht, or someone very much like him, who is talking.

For example, W. asks: "Can we change Shakespeare?" Rather sagely Brecht replies as B.: "It seems to me that we can change Shakespeare if we are able to change him."

Still, even if this symposium brushed in from memory seems rather stilted, it gives us an idea of what Brecht was driving at in his adaptation of *Coriolanus*. Referring to the plebeians, he asks: "Do they win their war against Marcius?" and has the answer served up by the letter R.: "In our theater, definitely."

The conclusions of this tetralogue are summed up at the end. R. asks: "Do you think that all this and the rest can be found in the play?"

Brecht, who is said to have been shrewd, answers: "Found in and read into."

P. is eager to know: "Is it because of this insight that we wish to put on the play?"

Brecht is confident in his aesthetics: "Only in part. We wish also to have, and to pass on to others, the pleasure of dealing with a piece of history that has been thoroughly elucidated. And the experience of dialectics."

This aim, if we are not too demanding, was achieved: with the help of the adaptation, a didactic play can be set before the public; within specified limits the audience may feel called upon to participate in the thinking that goes on in the play; and there is no reason why the index finger which points out what's what and summons the audience to join in the thinking, should not wear a relatively aesthetic glove, for otherwise the experience of dialectic and the enjoyment of tragedy will be stifled in the musty atmosphere of a schoolroom; but Coriolan must not be allowed to say what Coriolanus could. To Rome, which banished him, he said: "I banish you!"

Bertolt Brecht adapted this tragedy, which has still lost none of its sting, in 1952 and 1953. The period when he was working on it takes in the fateful date: June 17th. While Brecht, leaning on Livy, was racking his brains to figure out how to provide the plebeians, whom Shakespeare arms only with staves and clubs, with more effective weapons, the construction workers of Stalin-Allee revolted, unrehearsed and unarmed, to protest against the increased production norms, as in other days the plebeians rose against the prohibitive price of grain. These events suggest a play that might be entitled: "The Plebeians Rehearse the Uprising." Place: A theater in East Berlin. Someone who is addressed as "Boss" by his assistants and the actors, is rehearsing *Coriolan,* Act I, Scene 1, the uprising of the plebeians, and is trying to prevent a note of futility and comic sadness from creeping into his uprising.

We know that while the revolt in East Berlin and the provinces constituting the German Democratic Republic was going on, Brecht did not interrupt his rehearsals. He was, in fact, not rehearsing *Coriolan* but Strittmatter's *Katzgraben.* But the case of Brecht and the case of Sir Walter Raleigh seem to encourage the falsification of theatrical history and of English-Roman history for the benefit of historical drama.

Very well then: news of the uprising on Stalin-Allee filters into the theater where *Coriolan* is being rehearsed, conveyed first by stagehands, then by delegations from the construction workers, who disturb the Boss and the rehearsal.

We know that Bertolt Brecht took an attitude of wait-and-see toward the uprising of June 17th. His revolutionary experience had been the Spartacist uprising. The young Brecht wrote *Drums in the Night.* For him revolutionary German workers always bore the name of Kragler.

In my play the construction workers, who interrupt the Boss's rehearsals, ask this same Boss for support. They believe on the one hand that the celebrated dramatist and producer, as his plays and his ways indicate, is a friend of the people, and on the other hand that he is somebody whom the government supports and tolerates as a display of cultural property, or as a kind of privileged court jester.

We know that no authentic version of Bertolt Brecht's written statements about the revolt of the workers has thus far been published. His heirs and his publishing house have kept these documents under lock and key.

In my play the construction workers ask the Boss for a signed statement, for his signature carries a good deal of weight. They want him to put their clumsy call for a general strike, which RIAS, the American radio station, was willing neither to rewrite nor to broadcast, into the kind of words which they, the construction workers, did not have at their command.

We know that Bertolt Brecht emerged without visible harm from the workers' revolt: he retired to Buckow and wrote such poems as *Der Radwechsel, Eisen,* and *Böser Morgen.* His Ensemble continued to play, he continued to be the cultural property and advertisement of a state to which, according to his passport, he did not belong.

In my play the Boss does not refuse out of hand to write the statement the workers hope for. He agrees to compose it as soon as the masons and carpenters have shown him exactly what happened at the beginning of the workers' revolt; he wishes to derive benefit from current events for his production of *Coriolan,* for his uprising of the plebeians. The construction workers talk about Ulbricht and Grotewohl; he talks about the tribunes Sicinius and Brutus. The workers discuss the increased norms; he stresses the importance of Sicilian grain deliveries for Rome. The workers quote him; he quotes Shakespeare. The workers invoke the authority of Marx; he invokes the authority of Livy. The workers try to win him over to their revolt; he uses the workers for the staging of his plebeian uprising. The workers are undecided about their future attitude; he, the theater Boss, is sure of his thesis: in his play the plebeians are victorious, while on the stage of his theater, which mirrors the revolt of the construction workers, the workers' revolt collapses. In history—for the seventeenth of June has become history—and in my play Soviet tanks bring about the collapse of the uprising. While the workers in the play appraise the tanks as a fate which cannot be resisted or at the most with stones, the theater Boss delivers an impromptu speech on the subject of whether and how tanks can be used on the stage: as usual, everything turns to theater in his hands; slogans, speaking choruses, whether to march in columns of ten or twelve, everything becomes for him an aesthetic question: a man of the theater, serene and untroubled. Enjoyment of tragedy, *Coriolanus* and *Coriolan.* Two tribunes of the people and two assistants of the Berliner Ensemble. Blindfolded fate and manipulated partisanship. Grain prices and increased production norms. Construction workers and plebeian uprisings. A public place in Rome and the Government Building on Leipziger Strasse. Livy, Plutarch, and the S.O.P. of the RIAS radio station. History and its adaptation. Literary property and its owners. The national holiday and the Shakespeare Year: this play demands to be written.

The Plebeians Rehearse the Uprising

Cast of Characters

THE BOSS
ERWIN, Dramatic Adviser
VOLUMNIA
LITTHENNER, Assistant
PODULLA, Assistant

RUFUS
FLAVUS
BRENNUS
COCTOR
VARRO

KOWALSKI, Electrician

KOZANKA

HAIRDRESSER
FOREMAN
MASON
PLASTERER
WIEBE
DAMASCHKE
HOD CARRIER
ROAD WORKER
MECHANIC
CARPENTER
MOTORMAN
WELDER
MACHINIST
RAILROAD WORKER

Act I

(In the right foreground the director's desk, a comfortable armchair and a small table for the use of the BOSS, *with books and manuscripts on it. On the other side a tape recorder and a filing cabinet. The set suggests the Rome of Coriolanus.* LITTHENNER *drags in a dressmaker's dummy in the costume of Coriolanus.* PODULLA *follows, carrying scripts. They both look critically at Coriolanus.)*

LITTHENNER:

Hey, Whitey! Fly the houses to the grid.

(The drops, suggesting house fronts, are lifted)

PODULLA:

Why do we change Shakespeare?

LITTHENNER:

Because the Boss says we can.

PODULLA:

And we're still at it. But why him, why Coriolanus here? Coriolanus, proud to the point of arrogance, obstinate, unjust yet selfless. This monument of contradictions. This mountain, this colossus?

LITTHENNER:

The Boss wants to show that Coriolanus isn't indispensable.

PODULLA:

Singlehanded, he storms Corioli.

LITTHENNER:

A military specialist.

PODULLA:

No, a fate-ridden giant surrounded by plebeians.

LITTHENNER:

All the same, the plebeians have made up their minds to kill him. For fixing the grain prices.

PODULLA:

And he spits in their faces. He thinks the plebeians are ridiculous and the tribunes are nothing but puppets.

LITTHENNER:

The Boss' idea is to upgrade the plebeians and tribunes, give Coriolanus class-conscious enemies.

PODULLA:

He himself is enemy enough. Coriolanus defeats Coriolanus.

LITTHENNER:

With us the plebeians win out.

PODULLA:

I know his thesis. No muddleheaded insurrectionists—conscious revolutionaries. Can it be done?

LITTHENNER:

The first scene stands, I hope.

PODULLA:

Because he's having his plebeians rehearse in costume? The fable about the belly and the members has been thrown out three times.

LITTHENNER:

So we can keep on discussing it.

PODULLA:

We've been changing changes. I've been tinkering with this dummy for weeks. Even had to put this cloak through the wringer.

LITTHENNER:

Say what you please, the Boss has found his style again.

PODULLA:

Frayed leather and denim.

LITTHENNER:

The work clothes of a military specialist.

PODULLA:

Maybe this Coriolanus is good for scaring birds, but he certainly couldn't keep the plebs under his thumb or frighten the enemies of Rome. Coriolanus who wins battles as he breathes, whose pride moves nations and takes five acts to get its comeuppance . . .

LITTHENNER:

The Boss says that Coriolanus' sartorial simplicity is meant to underline his heaven-storming pride.

PODULLA (*laughing*):

Naturally. He's a careless dresser himself, he only changes his shirt when he has to.

LITTHENNER (*looking at him. After a pause*):

You don't suppose . . . ?

PODULLA:

No, I don't suppose.

(*Enter the* BOSS and ERWIN, *the dramatic adviser*)

BOSS:

Why this darkness?

PODULLA:

Work lights. Same as yesterday.

BOSS:

But this is a day of brightness. More light, Kowalski. Give us both pipes. In my mind and in Rome it's daylight. (*Facing the dummy*) Still too much ornament. (*He makes changes in Coriolanus' costume*)

Off with the gewgaws. He sets little store
By finery. Corpses, flames and leveled towns
Are his adornment, not flowing drapery.
That's how I see him, artisan of battle,

Blackmailing a nation until it believes
No one can ever replace him, Coriolanus—
Oh cult of personality!—unless we
Delete him. Do we really need him?
Forget what we did yesterday.
Wipe clean our mental slates. We know
Nothing. Now then, how does it begin?

ERWIN:
A mob! Plebeians armed with bats and clubs.
Hungry because the price of grain is climbing.
Resolved to kill the enemy of the people—
That's right, that's what it says—Coriolanus.

BOSS:
Who has well served his country!
The people can't check off his scars on all
The fingers of both hands.

ERWIN:
In Shakespeare there are twenty-seven of them.

BOSS:
The savior of his country. A whipping boy?

ERWIN: No, a hero!
The masons, bakers, ropers sing his praises . . .

BOSS:
And yet the selfsame ropers, masons, bakers
Are out to praise him with their clubs and bats,
Because he's sent the price of grain sky-high,
And olives too are out of sight.

PODULLA:
There's nothing about olives here.

LITTHENNER:
I don't see any olives in Livy or Plutarch either.

ERWIN:
Throw out the olives.

BOSS:

No, we need them as
An argument in the debate
Of the bakers, ropers, masons.

ERWIN:

The crux of the matter is they don't agree.
There's logic in Menenius's entrance.

BOSS:

Nothing is logical in this whole routine
If that old windbag with his dodge about
The body and the members can succeed, like
Some buttery nurse, in singing the revolt
To sleep before it's half begun.

ERWIN:

That old wives' lullaby saved the state.

BOSS:

You mean the belly, in other words, the nobles.

ERWIN:

Because he says the belly when he means
The state and the nobility.

PODULLA (*recites from Shakespeare*):

"There was a time when all the body's members
Rebell'd against the belly, thus accus'd it . . ."

ERWIN:

"That only like a gulf it did remain
I' the midst o' the body, idle and unactive,
Still cupboarding the viand, never bearing
Like labour with the rest, where the other instruments
Did see and hear, devise, instruct, walk, feel,
And, mutually participate, did minister
Unto the appetite and affection common
Of the whole body. The belly answer'd . . ."

BOSS:

And jabbers on with fancy metaphors . . .

ERWIN:

Telling the people, the agitated bones,
How aimlessly they'd flail the air
Without the state, that is, the belly,
That swallows up your lard and beans,
In fact the entire food supply.

BOSS:

To think that wretched, limping parable
Has earned itself a worldwide reputation!
Try it, I ask you, on welders and mechanics,
Just try it on a modern cable winder.

ERWIN:

Parable equals gullibility,
We'll gull the masses parabolic'ly.
For if I looked around me like a lighthouse,
(*To the assistants*)
I'd tickle you both pro and con
With the same blade of straw for argument . . .
Until some Mister Marcius came along—
Soon to be surnamed Coriolanus—
He beats about no bushes, speaks his mind,
And lures you with free grain, abundantly
Obtainable in the front battle line.
Even the people's tribunes, stupefied,
Stand looking round the vacant countryside.

BOSS:

Just stop the foolishness and play
The entrance of those newly elected idiots:
Brutus, Sicinius, or vice versa.

LITTHENNER:

"Was ever man so proud as is this Marcius?"

PODULLA:

"He has no equal."

LITTHENNER:

"When we were chosen tribunes for the people—"

PODULLA:

"Mark'd you his lip and eyes?"

LITTHENNER:

"Nay, but his taunts."

PODULLA:

"Being mov'd, he will not spare to gird the gods."

LITTHENNER:

"Be-mock the modest moon."

PODULLA:

"The present wars devour him. He is grown
Too proud to be so valiant."

BOSS:

Those disgruntled civilians will never be able to take the place of Coriolanus. We'll have to indoctrinate them, and that means change them.

LITTHENNER (*dead-pan*):

I hope you're not implying that Podulla and I might act like Sicinius and Brutus in a similar situation.

PODULLA:

Litthenner and I are definitely on the side of the people. What's more: thanks to your inspiration, this is a theater for the working class.

BOSS:

Let's be fair. Thanks to the subsidy we get from the government.

PODULLA:

Which is a government of the working class.

BOSS:

You've forgotten the peasantry. That calls for self-criticism; remember, they've promised us a new theater.

PODULLA:

Very well: the government of the first German workers' and peasants' state.

BOSS:

But even with the revolving stage they've promised us, my theater won't be a peasant theater.

ERWIN:

Words of wisdom. Put them on tape.

BOSS:

Where are those characters? Rufus, Flavus, Coctor, and so on. Late? Here we're rehearsing the revolution and the plebeians are late! Symbolism? No, plain sloppiness. Go look. No, stay here. Let's hear the new recording. We can't just sit here waiting. Lights!

LITTHENNER (*rummaging in the filing cabinet, holds out an index card*):

This one?

BOSS (*reading*):

"Grumbling housewives outside a government store. Slogans whispered by the delegates of the People's Light Bulb Factory in the May Day parade. — Whispering and Grumbling."

ERWIN:

What's the use of all this hocus-pocus?

BOSS:

Where else can we find the sound effects of a German workers' uprising? — And now go get me those plebeians. (LITTHENNER *and* PODULLA *exit*)

(*The tape is played. In the general hubbub words and half sentences can be distinguished: "Waiting three hours for two pounds of potatoes. Lousy planning. Eat the seed potatoes themselves. Late deliveries. And what about the spring potatoes? The bigshots got nothing to worry about. Potatoes. Ever since Stalin. No light bulbs, no potatoes. As long as Billygoat. Potatoes, potatoes. Damn Russians, feeding our potatoes to their pigs. To keep up their Five-Year Plan. But no consumer goods. They even export our potatoes. Wait till I meet Billygoat, I'll tell him. Potatoes*

. . . potatoes . . ." The BOSS *turns down the volume and speaks above the sound*)

All I hear is revolutionary demands for potatoes.

ERWIN:

They should have had a tape like that in November 1918.

BOSS:

Grumblers. Amateur revolutionaries. My plays are full of them. When they hear machine guns, they run.

ERWIN:

But don't forget *Spartacus* was your first successful play. (*Grinning*) Revolutionaries and moonlight.

BOSS:

Even Liebknecht and Luxemburg were romantics.

ERWIN:

And what were you? An undernourished anarchist with a guitar and talent.

BOSS (*laughs softly*):

It was a productive period though. The lines came bubbling. We argued all night. Should the revolution be classical or romantic?

ERWIN:

But in the end you came around to the aesthetic principle.

BOSS:

Marx himself stressed it.

ERWIN:

And Lenin says revolution should be practiced like an art.

BOSS:

Exactly. That's why we're putting on a didactic play. Instruct the public. Our indoctrinated tribunes will show the plebeians how you make a revolution and how you don't. —Or maybe something new and timely? Drop Coriolanus? Or go back to poetry? Short intimate poems. With trees in them. Maybe silver poplars.

(*He turns up the volume on the tape. The potato motif*

is repeated until the tape ends and a voice announces matter-of-factly: "End of tape. Beginning of a workers' uprising for Coriolanus *rehearsals, Scene One."* LITTHENNER, PODULLA, *and the five plebeians enter from the rear*)

ERWIN:

Silver poplars? Do my ears deceive me? Did you mention trees?

BOSS:

It won't happen again.

ERWIN:

If there's any demand for poems, it's for poems about potatoes.

BOSS (*sarcastically*):

Winter potatoes?

ERWIN (*with mock gravity*):

Spring potatoes.

BOSS:

All right, seed potatoes. — More light, Kowalski. Rome by daylight!

(*The assistants and plebeians are still standing in a group. The plebeians are holding clubs and sledge-hammers. They whisper, some with excited gestures, others with subdued embarrassment*)

LITTHENNER:

That can wait. We'll see. Anyway, the rehearsal comes first.

PODULLA:

Act One, Scene One. A street in Rome. The tape's running.

BOSS:

No private conversation, please.

(*The plebeians arrange themselves in groups*)

RUFUS:

"Before we proceed any further, hear me speak."

FLAVUS:

"Speak, speak."

RUFUS:

"You are all resolv'd rather to die than to famish?"

FLAVUS, COCTOR, VARRO, BRENNUS:

"Resolv'd! Resolv'd!"

RUFUS:

"First, you know Caius Marcius is chief enemy to the people."

FLAVUS, COCTOR, VARRO, BRENNUS:

"We know't, we know't."

BRENNUS (*leaps forward*):

Boss! There's something cooking in town.

RUFUS:

"Let us kill him, and we'll have corn at . . ."

VARRO:

Stop the show. I could hardly get through. They're marching ten abreast.

BOSS:

The usual parade. And now your lines if you please.

BRENNUS:

Coming, Boss. See! Locking arms, like a chain.

COCTOR:

They're not singing. You can hear their wooden clogs.

BRENNUS:

I almost wanted to join them.

FLAVUS:

I had to catch him by the belt.

VARRO:

Why don't we close up shop? Tomorrow's another . . .

BOSS:

And because of the usual parade, you want us to . . . ?

BRENNUS:

It's not the usual, Boss. Their faces are different today. And the women on the sidewalks, crumpling their handkerchiefs.

LITTHENNER:

I move that we stop the sound tape . . .

BOSS:

We and the tape will listen and observe how unusually they're marching today and how different the faces of the marchers are. We'll learn from those faces.

VARRO:

A lot of them are laughing, that's unusual.

COCTOR:

Some of the faces are serious. But not peevish as usual on such occasions, they're almost beautiful.

ERWIN:

Fine. Make a note: the beautiful seriousness of the plebeians.

BRENNUS:

Exactly. It makes you want to be down there marching with them, no matter where to and why, with whom and against whom.

BOSS:

No plan, no logic. You can't make a revolution with feeling.

RUFUS:

No weapons. Only briefcases on one side and bicycles on the other.

BOSS:

Who cares? Let them ride their bikes somewhere else and stop obstructing our merry rehearsal with their beautiful serious faces! Let's have that scene again. (*The plebeians hesitate*) Go ahead.

(*The* BOSS *goes back to his desk. The plebeians take their positions. The rehearsal begins. The actress who is to play*

VOLUMNIA *enters, passing through the group of plebeians. She is wearing a spring overcoat*)

RUFUS:

"Before we proceed any further, hear me speak."

FLAVUS:

"Speak, speak."

BOSS:

Is this a railroad station?

VOLUMNIA:

What? Rehearsing?

PODULLA:

Want me to stop?

ERWIN:

Yes, stop the tape.

BOSS:

No, let it run.

VOLUMNIA (*turns off the tape recorder*):

I do not wish to speak on tape.
(*To the* BOSS)
Well? Isn't it going as if by plan?
And it began spontaneously, without plan.

BOSS:

You mean the play, Scene One?

VOLUMNIA:

I'm speaking of the uprising, do you hear, the people!

BOSS:

And so am I. Look, here we are in Rome.
The people are rising up like amateurs . . .
But mother of our hero Coriolanus,
This scene, respected friend, is not
What's being rehearsed today.

VOLUMNIA:

Then I'm disturbing you?

BOSS:

That's right, disturbing.

VOLUMNIA:

But suppose the disturbances increase,
Suppose they rut and buck and whelp
Till one becomes a thousand.
Suppose we're not in Rome today
Or in King James's London,
But in Berlin, and half the city—
The Eastern half, I mean, our people—
Suppose all East Berlin should come disturbing,
Hissing, demanding,
And shut your theater down.

BOSS:

That smacks of Puritans;
But since, as you yourself just said,
This isn't Shakespeare's London—
Poor Shakespeare! Taking plague as a pretext,
They often shut him down—
My theater will stay open.
At worst we'll have some broken windowpanes.

VOLUMNIA:

I've never been afraid. This time I am.
Down there the people's rage is boiling over
And here we're stirring up theater dust . . .

BOSS:

Oh unrehearsed incompetence!

VOLUMNIA:

The people have risen.

BOSS:

Yes, yes, I know. Spontaneously!

VOLUMNIA:

They're serious.

BOSS:

If only that were true!

VOLUMNIA:

They've got accounts to settle.

BOSS:

I'll help them count.

VOLUMNIA:

They'll hang us all, you, him and me
From the gallery. To them we're bigshots,

BOSS:

I'll teach them the classic way to tie a slip knot.

VOLUMNIA:

Your skin has grown as thick as ox's hide.

BOSS:

Would you rather I had gooseflesh?

VOLUMNIA:

Like a broad river flow the angry masses,
Plowing the streets and shrinking tight the squares.
I saw them coming.

BOSS:

Good. Tell us all about it.

VOLUMNIA:

I saw wide-gaping mouths and whites of eyes.
The asphalt softened and the granite cracked.
I saw the skin on knuckles bursting. Blood.
A smell to curdle all the milk in the world.
Saw dust rise up in columns and screams congealed.
Maggots thought dead woke crawling in the meat.
Great palaces fell crumbling to their knees,
And fury struck with monumental fists.
They stormed the stairway. A baby carriage . . .

BOSS (*to Erwin*):

She's been at the movies, seeing Eisenstein.

VOLUMNIA:

. . . and placards waved above their heads,
And on them cried in bold hoarse lettering:
FOR PROPERTY.

FOR THE EXPROPRIATION OF THE OTHERS.
FOR THE NATURAL DISORDER OF THINGS.
FOR . . .

BOSS:

You've borrowed that from me. Every last word.
You always seem to find the right quotations.
One night I heard you dream quotations in
Your sleep. Please, comrade. Be yourself.

VOLUMNIA:

You won't believe me.

BOSS:

Every word's rehearsed.

VOLUMNIA:

All right. Be wily. Get on with your rehearsal.
Before the day is out the masons will
Be here and wall you up with bricks and mortar.

(*Three masons appear rear, dressed in white and carrying briefcases*)

BOSS:

They're here already, smelling of fresh lime.

(*They approach hesitantly. The* FOREMAN *compares the faces with a postcard-size picture. The light dazzles him*)

FOREMAN:

You're the boss here, aren't you?

BOSS:

I trust you haven't come here for my autograph.

MASON:

We only wanted to be sure.

PLASTERER:

You see, we think you're a great man. Big name.

BOSS:

My greatness and my name have a desk at home. When I sit there, I have a lovely view of the cemetery.

MASON:

You stand for something. Can't get around it. Everybody listens to you.

FOREMAN:

That's why we've come. We're a kind of delegation.

PLASTERER:

They picked me because on shop picnics I sometimes get up and make a little . . .

MASON:

So we said to ourselves: He's our man. Made a safe place for himself. He always gets what he wants. He's the man, he can help us.

FOREMAN:

Anyway: we're from Stalin-Allee.

BOSS (*standing up*):

And you want to start a revolution?

FOREMAN:

Revolution is going too far.

PLASTERER:

It's only about the norms.

MASON:

They are too high. And we're against.

BOSS:

Against? And what are you for?

FOREMAN:

What we're for? To get our norms re- . . .

BOSS:

Whose norms?

MASON:

The masons' norms, of course.

BOSS:

And not the welders' norms? Or the glaziers' norms?

PLASTERER:

Right now we're speaking for ourselves,
But if the welders and the glaziers . . .

MASON:

Who also have excessive norms to meet . . .

PLASTERER:

If they and the cable winders too,
If Buna, Leuna, and the uranium mines,
If all the boys from Bitterfeld and Halle,
From Magdeburg and Halberstadt
Are with us in being against . . .

BOSS:

Which isn't certain.

MASON:

Well, we masons anyway.

PLASTERER:

And if we all present the same demands
At the same time, on the same day . . .

BOSS:

And there are always malcontents.

PLASTERER:

Exactly, Boss. Well, then, then . . .

BOSS:

Well, then it's plain, there'll be a revolution.

FOREMAN:

No, revolution's going too far,
But maybe we could draw up a petition,
A statement . . .

MASON:

Or a manifesto maybe . . .

FOREMAN:

Nothing too long or radical . . .

PLASTERER:

Polite but firm: We are against . . .

FOREMAN:

But then we don't know what to say, see, Boss—
We only know the trade we've learned. But you . . .

MASON:

. . . They all say go ask him, he knows
The boys up top. And they know him . . .

PLASTERER:

. . . You're internationally known, you're, well . . .
A name to reckon with.

FOREMAN:

We've chewed the fat enough. Here's pen and paper.

(*The* BOSS *holds the paper up and examines it against the light.* ERWIN *is standing beside him*)

BOSS:

Has it ever struck you how a few years' use
Can drain a word—like "norms"—of meaning?

ERWIN:

That's how it was with the price of grain in Rome,
Bread came to be a pure abstraction.

BOSS:

My father was in the paper business,
But before I write I want to know.

ERWIN:

Which means, he wants to trust you like good friends.

BOSS:

Forget the price of grain. Give norms the floor.
Exit Rome. Enter Berlin.

ERWIN:

He's warming up.

PLASTERER:

What did I tell you? See, he's writing.

MASON:

Go on, he'll discuss us deaf and blind.
Discussion—that's his racket.

FOREMAN:

Our orders were to stay here till
He'd written something.

MASON:

That guy'll never write.

FOREMAN:

I say he will.

PLASTERER (*to the* MASON):

You want to bet . . . ?

(*With the last sentences the masons have taken a few steps backward. The plebeians exit left.* VOLUMNIA *goes up to the* BOSS)

VOLUMNIA (*trying to control herself*):

Hm, playing the Chinese sage again. So unworldly, so serene. Those people out there have suddenly realized that Stalin is dead. Dead and gone.

BOSS:

But his pictures are still all over the place as big as a house. — Go look in the storeroom. There must be some scraps we can use. A little experiment will show how much they've understood. Paste up the pieces. Don't spare the crape.

(LITTHENNER *and* PODULLA *exit*)

There must be some way of salvaging this morning.

VOLUMNIA:

They need help. They're convinced that the right words from you . . .

BOSS:

Do you believe in amulets to ward off colds?

VOLUMNIA:

A few words from you will give their stammering meaning.

BOSS:

Too much pointing crimps the fingers.

(PODULLA *and* LITTHENNER *come back with pieces of a picture of Stalin*)

VOLUMNIA:

What's the sense in this experiment? Whom do you want to test? Us? The masons? Or yourself?

BOSS (*slyly*):

It's my old trouble, curiosity. I'm curious to know which will come off better in the end: nature or my theater. No, put Coriolanus on the sidewalk. They'll do nicely together. (*Goes toward the masons*) So you were checking in as usual? At about seven o'clock? (*Calling upward*) Hey, Kowalski. Give us the other pipe. It's broad daylight.

FOREMAN:

In the summer we start at half past six.

ERWIN:

Put up a scaffolding.

BOSS:

No, just some suggestion.

ERWIN:

But at least there should be a sign saying: This is the construction site of the great Stalin's magnificent small-windowed avenue.

BOSS:

The picture says more than enough.

PLASTERER:

If you don't mind my putting in my two cents' worth: There's a loudspeaker not far from the job. And from morning to night it bawls: Build the future! Build the future!

MASON:

That's all very well, but we want something in writing, and we want it quick.

BOSS:

I'm working on it. — But how did it begin?

Mortar was being mixed, cement prepared;
Was it before or after breakfast?

FOREMAN:

No, we were eating breakfast. Word got round.
The boys from C-Block South came over,
But we of Block 40 were in the know,
We'd talked it over a few days ago
At one of our shop picnics and decided
That if this and that should happen, we . . .

PLASTERER:

And then somebody set up a barrel,
The kind they use for shipping lime . . .

BOSS:

Let's have a barrel. We'll imagine the lime.
No barrel? Well, then borrow some prop from Rome.

(*A truncated column is rolled in*)

PLASTERER:

And on the barrel stood old Hans—
A hod carrier. Quiet fellow. Never talks.
(*On the column*)
But this time, stripped to the waist, because the sun . . .

FOREMAN:

He spent four years in jail in Adolf's day.

PLASTERER:

Shouting: Comrades, attention please . . .

MASON (*pushes the* PLASTERER *off the pillar and jumps up*):

We've had enough play-acting. Does it make sense
To put on puppet shows for his amusement
While out in front they're marching ten abreast,
Arms locked and shouting: Comrades,
Comrades, join us!

PLASTERER *and* FOREMAN:

We want to be free men!

MASON:

All right, Boss, how's that statement coming?

(*Jumps down from the column*)
He's writing something. Is it for us?

FOREMAN:
Sh— Don't disturb him.

PLASTERER: He's fighting it out inside.

MASON:
He can do that tomorrow. The fire's today.

BOSS (*writing*):
Of course I'm writing for you. Everything I've ever written has been for you. But you forgot how to read before you even left school.

MASON:
Even if it's cardboard, I've got to do it. (*Starts battering the picture*)

BOSS (*stands up*):
But to the point: How many marchers have you got? Rough estimate?

FOREMAN:
About twenty thousand.

BOSS:
And now they'll run along home.

MASON:
Oh no, they won't! (*Goes on smashing*)

PLASTERER:
Maybe your doubts are justified, but this time we're in earnest.

MASON:
Haven't you got something to hit it with? (*Tears chunks out of the picture*)

PLASTERER:
That's enough, Karl.

FOREMAN (*to the* MASON *severely*):
No excesses, remember. (*To the* BOSS) In good order as we came from our jobs, unpolitically, without flags, not as

agitators but as human beings, we're going to march on the government quarter.

BOSS:

Just what I meant: unpolitically, without flags, and definitely as human beings, you're going to march straight back where you came from.

MASON:

Mustache is gone. Haven't you got a picture of Billygoat? The old Siberian goat?

ERWIN (*to* PODULLA):

Stop that tape recorder. Better go easy on our supplies.

(VOLUMNIA *takes the* BOSS *aside*)

VOLUMNIA:

You're out of contact with the people.
You expect them to scatter in confusion
The way they did in 1918, when you were twenty.

BOSS (*waves her aside*):

All revolutionaries, if you please
Keep off the grass and mind the shrubs and trees.

VOLUMNIA:

The workers' mentality has changed.

BOSS:

Yes, so I see. Today they beat up cardboard.

VOLUMNIA:

They've been indoctrinated. They know their worth.

BOSS:

If they're even worried about pictures,
Ask them about the grass. And ask them whether
They've made a plan and who their leader is.
(*Jumps up*) Have you occupied the radio?
Called a general strike? And what
About the Vopos? Looking the other way?
Taken precautions against Western agents?
And have you reassured the Soviets?
Have you made it clear that socialism stays?

And now suppose they send in tanks,
The model you are all familiar with.

FOREMAN:

Tanks? Tanks? Why tanks? We are unarmed.

MASON:

He means the Russkis. Suppose they send in tanks?

BOSS:

Which isn't certain, but it's possible.

FOREMAN:

Well, if the Russians come . . .

BOSS:

What then?

Before this ends in panic flight, in rout,
Look round you, comrades, find the back way out. —
And here come reinforcements. More petitions.
Better go home and give your wives a hand,
Help with the dishes, drive in lots of nails.
There's always something loose around the house. –
Beat it! Go home! And put your slippers on.
(*He turns brusquely away*)
Work lights, Kowalski. (*Half-darkness*)

(*Enter from the left the* CARPENTER, *the* ROAD WORKER, *the* HOD CARRIER, *the* MOTORMAN, *and the* MECHANIC *with a bicycle. The masons and workers form a group*)

MASON:

They're traitors.

VOLUMNIA (*indicating the Coriolanus dummy*):

This fellow's skin is rubbing off.

CARPENTER:

What is all this about? Is he supposed
To be a friend of the proletariat?

VOLUMNIA:

Have you turned Coriolanus?

BOSS:

I can't. I won't. You hear me? Nothing doing!

VOLUMNIA:

Are you his mouthpiece? Find the back way out!

BOSS:

Give them sausage. Give them bottled beer.

MASON:

These guys are hopeless.

ERWIN:

No, have paience.

VOLUMNIA:

Tell me, are you one mind with Coriolanus?

PODULLA:

Where is my text? Pride is always pride.

ERWIN:

Don't take it all so seriously.

HOD CARRIER:

You mean we're just kidding around?

BOSS:

Should I be diplomatic, should I lie?

LITTHENNER:

He can't go against nature.

BOSS:

"Am I to stammer now, forsaken by my lines?"

PODULLA:

But Rome demands it, Coriolanus. Leap!

BOSS:

"Like a dull actor now
I have forgot my part and I am out . . ."
Give me the book. What does he say next?
(*Takes* PODULLA'S *book*)

MOTORMAN:

What does he want? Applause? Egg in his beer?

BOSS (*kneels down*):

Must Coriolanus fall upon his knees:
"O Mother, Mother!" (*The workers laugh*)

ERWIN (*explaining to the workers*):
You see, those lines are out of Shakespeare's play;
And look at her, his mother Volumnia.
She's winding up. Looks like a monologue.

(VOLUMNIA *raises the* BOSS *up. The workers come closer*)

VOLUMNIA:
"There's no man in the world
More bound to 's mother, yet here he lets me prate
Like one i' th' stocks." (*Loudly*) Here's my advice to you,
Boss, take them as they are. Not so demanding!
If it's the custom here in Germany
For rebels to keep off the grass and treat
The People's flowerbeds with mild respect,
Never mind. Let them be mild and circumspect.
(*Standing with the masons*)
There's something else that's harder on these people
Than norms and prices, watery beer
And absence of potatoes. It's their thick tongues.
It won't come out, that's all. It won't come out!
All they can say is "norms. Too much, too high."
But you, though never a proletarian
Despite your cap, you've got the gift of gab.
Lord, what a manifesto you could write,
With forest glades of exclamation marks!
Then they'd be heard though they respect the grass.
It would be known: they still keep off the grass
Today, but when they stop respecting
The grass and the municipal flowerbeds,
When scissors threaten Billygoat and his chin-whiskers . . .

HOD CARRIER:
We're only demanding what's right and proper.

FOREMAN:
Right! We need his name. — Here! (*Points to the paper*)

BOSS:
You build walls. I write. Straight walls—straight sentences. Who can build them without difficulty? A minute ago I

thought a manifesto was shaping up; but now that I say it over, it smacks of elegy. (*Pushes the paper away*) Who'd benefit but poetry? (*He starts to leave, the* MASON *stops him*)

MASON:

And what about our paper? Want it to rot?

CARPENTER:

If he can't think of anything, he should say so.

PLASTERER:

Go on! The government's building him a new theater.

ROAD WORKER:

That's why he won't do anything for us.

MASON:

They're all the same. Bigshots! They're all the same. What are we waiting for? (*He starts to leave*)

VOLUMNIA:

Wipe off that sheepish grin. Do something!

BOSS:

Wherever I look: kneaders of dough, who want to bake a shining hero out of me. (*He exits*)

ERWIN:

You didn't convince him.

VOLUMNIA:

And he wants to be convinced with our help. It's up to us.

MASON (*calls after them*):

You mean we've got to dance for him some more?

ERWIN:

Great bastions are seldom taken at the first try.

(VOLUMNIA *and* ERWIN *exit after the* BOSS)

CURTAIN

Act II

(The workers and plebeians are standing in separate groups. PODULLA *by the tape recorder)*

COCTOR:
Your clothes are wringing wet. You'll catch your death.

BRENNUS:
Wouldn't you like to take them off?

CARPENTER:
Don't worry. We won't grow moss around here.

MOTORMAN:
They'll put you into costume.

PLASTERER:
Wait and see. They're going to make us historical.

ROAD WORKER *(pointing to the plebeians and* PODULLA*)*:
Are they here to keep an eye on us?

MASON:
No, they're just a bunch of hams. — You've been in West Berlin?

ROAD WORKER:
They won't stir a finger. They're yellow.

CARPENTER:
And the minister, what's his name . . .

ROAD WORKER:
They've written us off.

CARPENTER:
. . . told them not to do anything rash.

ROAD WORKER:

Yes, written us off.

CARPENTER:

That's what the minister said.

(LITTHENNER *enters from the right*)

PODULLA:

Any news of the Boss?

LITTHENNER:

First he wanted to go home and sit in his rocking chair.

PODULLA:

That's nice.

LITTHENNER:

He was outvoted. She sat down at the organ and pulled all the stops: Where's your famous patience? You don't even know what's going on. You can't prove a thing. All prejudice. Sheer pigheadedness!

PODULLA:

Then what? Did he beat his breast?

LITTHENNER:

Then when Erwin came out with some facts, he . . .

PODULLA:

Go on.

LITTHENNER:

. . . well, first he hid behind a cigar. Then he said "Good," and then very quietly: "I'll prove you're mistaken . . . but never mind. Let them talk. Let them get it off their chests—to our profit."

PODULLA:

We're going to have our hands full.

LITTHENNER:

And finally he wrapped it all up in a parable. Listen to this: A theoretician was sitting at his desk. A tiger came in and was going to eat him.

PODULLA:

I suppose the theoretician said: Wait, tiger, until I stand up.

LITTHENNER:

Sitting, he said to the tiger: Before you put theory into practice, tell me how many teeth you have, explain the system of their arrangement; and I should also like to know what aesthetic principle governs your haunches.

PODULLA:

The tiger left the theoretician time to say all that?

LITTHENNER:

The tiger pondered a long while, at a loss for an answer.

PODULLA:

And in the end he slunk away like a lamb.

LITTHENNER:

Wrong. He ate him without a theory.

PODULLA:

That's a lie.

LITTHENNER:

All right, I'll tell you: From that day on the tiger was the theoretician's disciple; he became more and more ashamed of his ignorance.

PODULLA:

And that was the moral of the Boss's story?

LITTHENNER (*turns to the workers*):

The Boss has seen the light. When he comes back here, open up. Tell him everything you know, everything you think, everything you ever thought. Omit nothing. He's interested in the weather too. Even your private affairs are relevant. He knows you all have families.

FOREMAN (*with reserve*):

We'll say what needs to be said.

CARPENTER (*points to the plebeians*):

In front of those apes?

ROAD WORKER:

Roman rags. All camouflage.

CARPENTER:

How do we know there aren't any stool pigeons in among them?

RUFUS:

And how do we know there are real masons in those work clothes, and not Western agents?

MASON:

I'm getting sick of that guy. Say, comrade stool pigeon, where can we hear you sing?

PODULLA:

Take it easy, boys.

MASON:

At Soviet headquarters or in Billygoat's private office?

FLAVUS:

Provocateur. Paid agent!

MASON:

Party bosses! Parasites!

PODULLA:

Stop it.

CARPENTER:

Bureaucrats!

PODULLA:

Stop it, I say.

CARPENTER:

Apparatchiks!

RUFUS:

Throw the bastard out if he isn't willing to discuss.

ROAD WORKER:

If anybody's going to be thrown out of here . . .

LITTHENNER:

Let's not get spontaneous.

CARPENTER:

Let's go! Before they turn us in.

(*The* CARPENTER, *the* ROAD WORKER, *the* MASON *on one side,* RUFUS *and* FLAVUS *on the other, come to blows. The rest of the workers and plebeians try to make peace*)

HOD CARRIER:

Don't let them provoke you. Our enemies are someplace else.

BRENNUS:

Hold your people back.

FOREMAN:

Stop it, do you hear? Stop it!

PLASTERER:

No excesses! Remember, that's what we decided.

PODULLA:

If this is the practice, his theory was wrong.

(*The* BOSS *enters left, followed by* VOLUMNIA *and* ERWIN)

BOSS:

Now that I call class struggle. A drunken wedding
Between the plebs and proletariat.

ERWIN:

An exemplary image!

(*The brawl begins to break up*)

BOSS (*leaps in among the workers, grabs hold of them*):

Good! Do it again. The same position, please.
Here, you grab him and you punch him.
He ought to sweat, his tongue should be hanging out,
And you, look pained. His knee is in your groin!
Plebeians' rags inextricably mingled
With masons' white, sleeves, trouser legs.
This neck, this back, they're cracking,
Because that knee, that forearm . . . Apply the thumb!
And now hold still a second
Like statues, like Laocoön.

If only we could cast you all in bronze,
And put you on a pedestal with the
Inscription: Socialism, scorning pain
And muscle cramp— Well, what does socialism do?
Behold—it conquers! Well, that's that. And now,
Plebeians and proletarians, relax,
And tell me all about the uprising.
(*The group drifts apart*)

MASON (*to* FOREMAN):
No, you begin.

FOREMAN (*to the* BOSS):
You asked for it: well, this has been building up a long time over on Stalin-Allee. I've got three kids. The boy wants to be an electrician.

BOSS (*interested*):
What are your names?

MASON (*pushing forward*):
They've got nothing to do with it.

BOSS (*friendly*):
Why don't you sit down? Been on your feet since half past six.

(*The workers sit down side by side on a raised platform*)

PLASTERER:
Don't get us wrong: We of Block 40 had a reputation for militancy. Used to be a salesman. Went to retraining school. Class of '19.

MASON:
Class of '22. Rare article since the war. Yes, they've loosened up a little, like returning the property of fugitives from the Democratic Republic, who want to come back. But damn near everything from potatoes to safety pins is still rationed.

FOREMAN:
Still, the pressure's let up some. Even on the Church, so my wife tells me. — We're Protestants.

MASON:

But they've lowered the alcohol content of the beer and hiked up all the norms. — Protestant myself.

PLASTERER:

Same here. — The thing about the norms was in the *Tribune*. That's our union paper. It's against us. — Fought in France, the Balkans, and the Ukraine.

MASON:

It said the norms were going up. Voluntarily and right away.

FOREMAN:

Ten percent on Stalin-Allee.

CARPENTER:

All over. — I was in the armored infantry. Five years in Siberia. Came back three years ago.

BOSS:

Then it started on your job?

FOREMAN:

On the dot of nine fifteen. I lived through Demyansk. Then the Kurland army.

MASON:

We guys from Block 40 with a placard. Eighty of us. Down with the norms, that's what it said. Wounded in the shoulder. Cold-storage medal.

PLASTERER:

The guys from C-Block South joined us.

FOREMAN:

The other blocks too. About fifteen hundred men.

PLASTERER:

They organized a speaking chorus:

Fellow masons, join us fast,
We want to be free men at last.

CARPENTER:

When there were no more masons to join us, we made a slight change:

Friends, Berliners, join us fast,
We want to be free men at last.

ROAD WORKER:
And then they all came running, even housewives.

CARPENTER:
But the dark-blue Vopos didn't move.

MOTORMAN:
And our crew said the same: No bloodshed!

THE WORKERS (*all talking at once*):
No bloodshed. Wounded three times. Bloodshed. Once in the lungs. No bloodshed. We in Demyansk. In two days half the company. And on the highway to Smolensk. You should have seen the mess at Kursk. And what about the Kuban bridgehead? Belly wounds. One, two, three, four.

BOSS:
Rufus, Varro, Coctor, Flavus, Brennus— There's our scene after the Volscian war.

(*The plebeians face the workers on the platform*)

RUFUS:
And now he's consul.

BRENNUS:
And we elected him.

FLAVUS:
And he hasn't even shown us his wounds.

COCTOR:
The law demands it.

VARRO:
We ought to contest his election.

RUFUS:
Then we revolt?

BRENNUS:
Against Coriolanus, yes.

RUFUS:
But not with arms. I'm fed up. I was wounded here . . . and here, when we drove Tarquin out.

VARRO:

At Corioli I charged straight into a phalanx of spears. Still, it was a victory.

COCTOR:

This missing finger was a present to the Sabines.

BRENNUS:

The fields of the Volscians drank my blood.

FLAVUS:

In the Alban Hills I lost a boot with contents.

RUFUS:

Before Antium our cohort fattened the vultures.

VARRO:

Antium? At Corioli we made breastworks out of corpses.

RUFUS:

Anything to add? Breastworks out of corpses. And you want us to take up arms again?

BOSS:

The veterans' reminiscences in both camps add up to the motto:

Kindly shoot above the trees.
We want our freedom, but no bloodshed, please.

FOREMAN:

That's right. — But there are some things we won't take lying down. When a civilian snapped our picture, we made him hand over the film.

BOSS:

Photographers will not molest
Workers assembled to protest.

You ought to carry signs proclaiming these dangerous truths.

VOLUMNIA:

There's too much method in your method.

MASON:

He's barring his windows same as the university. Intellectuals! Solidarity! We yelled. Our speaking choruses. It was a flop, same as here.

BOSS (*softly, emphatically*):

Maybe the students were listening with bated breath to a lecture about Lenin's letters to the Petrograd comrades, proving, with quotations from Marx, that revolution like war is an art.

ERWIN:

If the students hang back, you can hardly call it an uprising of the people.

MASON:

Does he think we're playing blindman's buff out there? Three thousand men!

CARPENTER:

When we got to the Government Building . . .

HOD CARRIER:

Which used to be the Air Ministry . . .

CARPENTER:

. . . they closed the gates. But we shouted—six thousand of us: Ulbricht or Grotewohl!

ROAD WORKER:

But they didn't come out. Neither one of them.

MOTORMAN:

And the sun beat down on us.

CARPENTER:

So some of us—we were about eight thousand in all—sat down on Göring's former sidewalk until Selbmann came out.

MECHANIC:

He's the heavy-industry guy.

PLASTERER:

He brought a table and a professor. The table was to climb on. But they had to help him up. (*He climbs up on the platform with the help of the workers*) Fellow workers! (*The workers laugh*)

MOTORMAN:

We're not *your* fellow workers!

CARPENTER:

That's what we said. And he said:

PLASTERER:

I'm a worker like yourselves. (*The workers boo*)

MASON:

You're a traitor to the working class!

PLASTERER:

Then he held out his hands and yelled: Look at my hands!

MASON, ROAD WORKER, CARPENTER:

Too fat! Too fat!

CARPENTER:

They're too fat.

MOTORMAN:

And the sun was shining on his fat hands until he pulled them in. (*The* PLASTERER *stays on the platform*)

CARPENTER:

So then we decided to set up another speaking chorus with a new slogan: The liberation of the workers can only come from the workers. Something like that.

MECHANIC:

But we couldn't agree whether it's Marx or Lenin. Or maybe Stalin.

PLASTERER:

Marx okay, but . . .

ROAD WORKER:

Anyway we didn't have a microphone.

FOREMAN:

There are plenty on Stalin-Allee. And so many loudspeakers it rings in your ears at night.

ROAD WORKER:

If we'd only brought them along.

MECHANIC:

That's what I always say: If you'd only.

BOSS:

If we'd only this! If we'd only that! They lament like Shakespeare's plebeians.

VOLUMNIA:

You'll be lamenting pretty soon: If I'd only this! If I'd only that! Friend, you too are mortal.

BOSS:

Did I ever claim this rehearsal was in heaven?

MASON (*pokes the* FOREMAN):

Do something, or we'll still be here next Sunday.

FOREMAN:

But then our Hans climbed up on the table. (*Motions the* MASON *to come down and helps the* HOD CARRIER *up*)

MASON (*to the* CARPENTER):

It was high time.

HOD CARRIER:

I'm a hod carrier on C-Block South.

PLASTERER:

He was stripped to the waist. He wasn't rough. He just swept Selbmann off the table, and the professor too.

HOD CARRIER:

And this is what I said: We haven't climbed down off our scaffolds to complain about the shortage of sardines. Nobody's griping because there are enough bicycle pumps to pump up a zeppelin, but no inner tubes. If you see us standing here in the heat, it's not just because the norms are too high and the alcohol content too low . . .

MASON *and* CARPENTER:

Beer without no alcohol,
Thank you, thank you, Grotewohl.

HOD CARRIER:

No, my friend, this here is a revolution, that's what I said.

FOREMAN:

And then we demanded the resignation of the government and free secret elections.

MASON:

Somebody said: Gen-er-al strike.

HOD CARRIER:

And that's why we're here. We've been over there at the radio.

FLAVUS:

In West Berlin, you mean?

RUFUS:

I get it. Stirred up by agitators.

MOTORMAN:

Don't be an ass. The Americans wouldn't have anything to do with us. They thought the Russians had sent us.

BRENNUS:

That's a fact. I was listening to the Western radio in the canteen. The only one that spoke was somebody from the West Berlin Trade Unions.

MASON:

Scharnowski?

HOD CARRIER:

But on the American station he couldn't say anything about a general strike. Oh no! That would be meddling in our internal affairs.

BRENNUS:

Of course not. What did I tell you?

FOREMAN:

And that's why we're here.

MASON:

Why we're still here.

MECHANIC:

Anyway, it started to rain.

MOTORMAN:

We're soaked. Even our sandwiches.

FLAVUS:

What if it keeps on raining?

RUFUS:

Yeah! Then what?

(*The workers do not answer*)

BOSS:

Do I have to think of everything? Litthenner, Podulla! Our guests are entitled to expect a certain minimum of consideration. Dry shoes and clothing. I won't have anybody catching pneumonia in my theater. Be sensible. Colds and grippe won't change the world. Here we'll keep out of the rain. Hang up your wet things. Put up a clothesline for our friends. Across the stage. (*The assistants and plebeians put up a clothesline across the stage. The workers hang their smocks up to dry*)

VOLUMNIA:

Have you noticed, Erwin? I smell social work.

ERWIN:

He always had a weakness for the Salvation Army.

VOLUMNIA (*to the* BOSS):

Next you'll be opening a soup kitchen.

BOSS:

The Shakespearean downpour is watering down a program that was soggy to begin with.

ERWIN:

And you want to give it sparkle.

BOSS (*to* VOLUMNIA):

Why can't you look at this from the practical side? Think of the picture, the image: a revolution wilted by the rain: a German revolution! (*Softly*) The heavens have done their thinking for them.

VOLUMNIA:

What a crumby aesthete you turned out to be!
(LITTHENNER *and a few plebeians distribute plebeian costumes among the workers*)
Well, now you've done it.
Turned workers into extras like a baker
Cutting his dough to make up Christmas cookies.
All right, don't listen. This time I'll say it softly:
From this day on, which cries out for socialism
As do we all, you, I and he—
Every mechanic, mason, carpenter
Will call you traitor if you don't bestir yourself.

ERWIN:

Then it's his duty to correct the picture
Before they print it up in East and West.

VOLUMNIA:

Here are the witnesses.

BOSS (*pointing to the dummy*):

Should I bribe them?
Should I, like this fellow in the forum, beg,
"Brag unto them, thus I did, and thus . . ."
Should I disguise my voice and play the bride,
And at the same time vaunt her maiden charms?
Look, see how chaste she is, without a blemish.
(*Plays the bride*)
Oh yes, indeed, I'm chaste as chaste can be.
She's fought for justice and for socialism
From childhood on.
Oh yes, I've fought for justice,
Those words, those flashes of her spirit,
Were like a light in darkness.
Yes, I lit
The world.
Reviled I was, and persecuted,
And threatened with death.
Oh yes, a hundred times.

Should I pick up their votes like cigarette butts
Here in the forum? (*To the dummy*)
What do *you* say, pal?
(*Quoting*)
"Show them the unaching scars which I should hide . . ."
(*Upward*)
Kowalski, dim the lights.
(*In the midst of the workers*)
Ah, my good friend, and you, my comrade!
Bold mason, proud, class-conscious motorman!
All you plebeians and proletarians!
Go home. Trot off in peace, and when you're gone,
Remember me kindly, please. I have deserved it.

MASON (*flabbergasted*):
Man, he's a riot. (*He bursts out laughing. One by one the other workers join in. The laughter builds up*)

BOSS (*to* VOLUMNIA):
Is that how I should speak? With tears in my eyes:
Beloved voices, vote for me?

VOLUMNIA (*with resignation to* ERWIN):
How about some coffee?

ERWIN:
It wouldn't hurt you to remember your Hegel.
(*He nods. She puts on water for instant coffee*)

VOLUMNIA:
He used to listen to me. This time you can mother him. (*She sits down*)

ERWIN:
He is being kind of childish.

BOSS:
What can I do? I can't stand revolutionaries who are afraid to walk on the grass.

ERWIN:
I don't know exactly what you mean by grass. But suppose they trample it flat, do you expect them to stop at grass?

Won't your theater lose its freshness too? They'll smash the seats for firewood. Democracy will cut dolls out of the curtain. They'll use our props for toys because first one, and then the pack, dared to walk on the grass.

VOLUMNIA:

Do you think they'll draw a line between the grass and your theater?

ERWIN:

They'll be blind. Or if they see at all, everything, your theater too will tempt them like luscious grass.

BOSS:

But the fact is that they keep off it. They pussyfoot around out there on their tiptoes, mumbling jingles. — But silly as their procession may be, we can get something out of it. For *Coriolanus* or for some play that's clamoring to be written. By showing what shouldn't be done, we make it clear what the revolution demands. (*To the* FOREMAN) You come to me and say: Do something for us. All right, I'll do something for you. With your help. I'll show you what you're doing out there. Let's assume the procession forms back there. We'll need placards with slogans in favor of order and against bloodshed. (*To the plebeians*) You boys can help them with the wording. Show us what you've learned, Litthenner. (*To the* FOREMAN) We'll want your speaking choruses. You know what it's all about, so don't start fighting again. (LITTHENNER *exits with the plebeians and workers. The* BOSS *motions* PODULLA *to come close*) And now, Podulla, let's put our revolutionaries in a difficult situation. Here we'll have grass—and here—and over there. Mark it off. (*Calls upward*) And give us light—Sunday light.

PODULLA:

This is Wednesday, Boss. (*He exits*)

VOLUMNIA (*Pours coffee. To the* BOSS):

Want some?

BOSS:

To give you the pleasure of hearing me say yes: Yes.

VOLUMNIA:

Still no sugar?

ERWIN:

As if he could change!

VOLUMNIA:

I can remember a time when he chewed the beans all night.

BOSS:

Besides, there's a football game over there on the weekend. Stuttgart-Kaiserslautern. Those things take people's minds off . . .

VOLUMNIA:

Off what? Off what? You need a new girl friend. Different color hair. Better ideas.

BOSS:

Weren't you getting me a cup of coffee?

VOLUMNIA:

Here. (*Hands him a cup. He drinks with gusto*)

BOSS:

We could order a case of beer. What do you say, Erwin?

ERWIN:

Good idea. And sandwiches.

(*In the rear* PODULLA *marks out the grass plots with the help of some stagehands*)

BOSS:

Right. Here's a canteen slip. And now observe! . . . I'm going to sign. (*He signs a slip and gives it to* PODULLA, *who goes out.* VOLUMNIA *comes close to the* BOSS)

VOLUMNIA:

Is that all?

BOSS:

What do you suggest?

I wash my hands. Why bother to roll stones
That roll themselves—downhill.

VOLUMNIA:

You say that now. But think back, man.
I found you in the gutter.

BOSS:

In the muck.
It wasn't bad. I'd made myself at home:
The brawl in Dresden, you remember?
The time with Pauli, the light heavyweight . . .

VOLUMNIA:

That's how I found you, fondling chaos,
Half starved, in love with nothingness,
Paddling about in misery. Aimless . . .

BOSS:

My course was right. Only the compass lied.

VOLUMNIA:

Say, Erwin, which is east? — Is it this way?
(*Points her thumbs in opposite directions*)
His course was right. Only our compass lied.
You poet!

BOSS:

You Duse of the barricades.

VOLUMNIA:

You parlor Marxist.

BOSS:

Fighting floozie!

VOLUMNIA:

You . . . you! . . . Why, I could . . .

BOSS:

You could? . . .
I could . . .

VOLUMNIA:

What could you, angel? Spit it out.

BOSS:

Stinker! My darling stinker.

VOLUMNIA:

Lover!

BOSS:

Comrade!

(*They embrace with loud laughter*)

ERWIN:

The old family record. I get a kick out of it every time. (*He joins in the laughter.* PODULLA *comes back and sits down by the tape recorder.* LITTHENNER *comes in from the left, followed by a chorus of plebeians carrying placards saying: "No Bloodshed," "Don't take pictures," "Keep order," "Keep off the grass." They post themselves at one side. The workers appear with signs saying: "Down with the Norms," "Out with Billygoat." They start their procession, which gets more and more confused because of their efforts to avoid the grass plots*)

LITTHENNER:

We've risen up in our town
In order to put Ulbricht down.

WORKERS:

Friends, Berliners, join us fast,
We want to be free men at last.

LITTHENNER:

Photographers have taken their places,
They want to snap the workers' faces.

CHORUS OF PLEBEIANS:

Photographers will not molest
Workers assembled to protest.

WORKERS:

Friends, Berliners, join us fast,
We want to be free men at last.

LITTHENNER:

When workers staunchly raise their heads,
They mustn't harm the flowerbeds.

CHORUS OF PLEBEIANS:

All revolutionaries, please
Keep off the grass and spare the shrubs and trees.

WORKERS:

Friends, Berliners, join us fast . . .

MASON (*pushes the signs aside and bursts out*):

Grass, grass, all I hear is grass. There isn't any in this town. Nothing but rubble, war damage, weeds! What are we, anyway? Clowns? Horsing around with his grass while our people down there! (*To the* BOSS) You . . . you . . .

CARPENTER:

Give it to him straight.

MASON:

I'll give it to him. You . . .

ROAD WORKER:

Somebody's got to tell him.

MASON:

Do you know what you are?

HOD CARRIER:

Give it to him good.

MASON:

You, you, you're a rotten, no-good, slimy, underhanded . . . you, you . . . I tell you, you're a rotten no-good . . .

BOSS (*serenely*):

I can't stand the suspense. You mean I'm a traitor to the working class. Is that it? (*To* PODULLA) That was an interesting crescendo. Let's hear it again. In the series of adjectives we have just heard, I wish to call your special attention to the formulation "rotten, no-good."

PODULLA:

Do you want the part about the grass?

BOSS:

"Clowns" is the cue. (PODULLA *turns on the tape recorder*)

THE TAPE:

Are we clowns? Horsing around with his grass while our people down there! You . . . you . . . Give it to him straight. I'll give it to him. You . . . Somebody's got to tell him. Do you know what you are? Give it to him good. You, you . . . you're a rotten, no-good, slimy, underhanded . . . you, you . . . I tell you. You're a rotten, no-good . . . I can't stand the suspense. You mean I'm a traitor to the working class. Is that it?

BOSS (*stops the machine*):

Not a bad trick, that repetition. How would it be—just by way of testing our invention and possibly improving on it—to throw in another "rotten no-good" between "slimy" and "underhanded"?

PODULLA:

You're a rotten, no-good, slimy, rotten, no-good, underhanded . . .

MASON (*to* PODULLA):

Shut up! (*To the* BOSS) You're a rotten no-good stinker.

CARPENTER:

He's hit the nail on the head.

MASON:

A stinker, that's what he is, a rotten, no-good . . .

LITTHENNER:

What do you think of that, Boss?

BOSS:

Not so good. Commonplace. A crescendo has to build up to something good. "Traitor to the working class" is a lot better than stinker. But neither touches me. Remember that vilification is a weapon. Your enemies have been wielding it with virtuosity for centuries. Why not learn from them? (*Points to the Coriolanus dummy*)

Whenever this man runs into a plebeian,

The gutter gurgles from his very entrails.
He talks of dogs, talks of dissentious rogues
Who rub their itch like lepers. In his mouth
Plebeians are no better than sewer rats.

CARPENTER:

What can we learn from that?

BOSS:

What? Lepers,
Rats! Dogs! You take it lying down?

CARPENTER:

They give
Us worse than that. It doesn't bother us.
You want to learn? Christ! Any stupid fool
Can rattle off a better list than that.
Class enemy. Agent of the Western Powers.

PLASTERER:

Class collaborator. That's more up to date.

CARPENTER:

Fascist. Old-fashioned, but still effective.

MOTORMAN:

And once, before I knew what the word meant,
Somebody called me an ob-jec-tiv-ist.

PLASTERER:

And how about capitulator?

HOD CARRIER:

Uprooted element!

PLASTERER:

Revisionist!
Saboteur, reactionary!

MASON:

Today, it's safe to bet, they're calling us
Provocateurs and putschists . . .

FOREMAN:

And deviationists and Western spies.

PLASTERER:

They've made a combination recently
Of saboteur and Western agent: Sabogent!

(*Laughter among the workers*)

BOSS:

You're right. Rats, dogs—one gets used to that. Objectivist? Capitulator? Paper bullets. Abstract stones that miss the mark. Wouldn't it be more effective to borrow from everyday life? For instance, our cherished habit of eating potatoes every day? — Potato eater. You lousy potato eaters! — Or your virility, there you're vulnerable! How about "weekend stallions"? Not bad: you weekend stallions, you! Or one might list your harmless leisure occupations: rabbit breeders, beer hall strategists, Sunday gardeners. Because that's exactly what you are: dangerous beer hall strategists. (KOZANKA *enters from the left. The* BOSS *resents the intrusion*)

BOSS:

Now what's the trouble? We're rehearsing here.

KOZANKA:

It's Kronstadt, man. It's counterrevolution.

FOREMAN:

We know that bastard.

KOZANKA:

The rats are coming up for air.

VOLUMNIA:

Why, it's the people's bard.

ERWIN:

Your worthy colleague.

KOZANKA:

From every sewer: counterrevolution.
We've got to put it down.

PLASTERER:

He's Billygoat's mouthpiece.

KOZANKA:
No discussion please. We need you.
Not just your name. Your tongue can help us too.
To you they'll listen. All I got was catcalls.

VOLUMNIA:
All want your help, the rebels want it and
The state as well. Ah! What power, coveted
By all, sits in this modest easy chair.

BOSS:
Kowalski, give us work lights again.

KOZANKA:
I tried to get their ears on Spittelmarkt,
I spoke almost politely, but they booed.

BOSS:
Let's see your eyes, Kozanka. Comrade,
It's jaundice. I prescribe a saltless diet.

KOZANKA:
There's worse to fear than diet. They're coming, Boss.
Demanding freedom. They've been brainwashed.

BOSS:
Then
Only the brainwashed feel the need of freedom?

KOZANKA:
They're marching this way, five, six columns of them.

BOSS:
The brainwashed mob, demanding freedom.

KOZANKA:
Provocateurs and putschists,
Fascist dogs and Western agents, coming
(*The workers laugh*)
To dynamite the House of Culture.

BOSS:
Why wouldn't they?

KOZANKA:

They're fifty thousand strong.

ERWIN:

Why, Kozanka, that's a good-sized audience you've attracted with your eloquence.

VOLUMNIA:

A literary triumph! Aren't you proud?

KOZANKA:

It's no joke this time, Boss. We'll have to quiet
Them down with iron words. We're only thirty
Here in the House of Culture. All unarmed.

ERWIN:

I hope so. Would a poet want to fire
On readers who, quotations on their lips—
"Build, build the future"—come here to applaud
The people's poet, shouting: "Solidarity!"

KOZANKA (*to* ERWIN):

That gag may be your last.

ERWIN:

I'd gladly see
It cut in marble.

KOZANKA:

They'll take their revenge,
Exacting tooth for tooth and eye for eye . . .

VOLUMNIA:

By showing his face, Kozanka has offended
Their eyes, and now his own eye itches.

KOZANKA:

Come out with me and speak to them.
You've got the eloquence, the wit
To stop them all, all fifty thousand
Victims of foreign agitators,
And send them home where they belong.

BOSS:

But that would be a bitter disappointment.
Those fifty thousand have come here to applaud you.
The West extols *my* writings to the skies,
The East takes pleasure in Kozanka's lies.

(*He turns away*)

KOZANKA:

I'd like to have that last remark in writing.

BOSS:

Everyone wants me to get out my pen.

KOZANKA:

But who supports your theater? Tell me that.

BOSS:

Everyone wants to milk me. First
The subjects, then the state itself.
I'm not your cow.

KOZANKA:

Who coddles you and puts up with your whims?
The formalism you call realism?
The West? Or is it the Democratic Republic?

BOSS:

We're very grateful to our noble patron.

KOZANKA:

That is, the state. Your patron is the state.

BOSS:

How could I ever forget the state! And now
Let's show our gratitude by buckling down.

KOZANKA:

The truth . . .

BOSS:

is concrete, this is a rehearsal.

KOZANKA:

What's a rehearsal when the toiling masses,
Ignoring their directors, start acting on their own?

BOSS:

Listen to me. The joys of love in bed,
Baptism soon, and later arduous death,
War, peace, all have to be rehearsed.
Football, the hunt, a game of cards,
Why, even chaos has to be rehearsed;
Hiccups, magician's tricks,
The saint tries out his miracles,
And we the rising of the plebs.
In this case now, the popular fury
Wants to be wed with civic spirit.
These people scorn to litter the streets
With sandwich papers while the battling masses
Assault the House of Culture and Town Hall.
No, no, the proper place for sandwich papers
Is the municipal trash can, with a slit
On top, and printed legibly, a sign:
"The people keep their city clean."
This is the kind of neat and civic conduct
We're planning to rehearse. — And now, lights please!

LITTHENNER:

So try to find some prop that looks like . . .

BOSS:

And what about that beer?

PODULLA:

It's here. And lots of sandwiches.

MECHANIC:

Good idea, a little snack would hit the spot.

(RUFUS *and* FLAVUS *bring in a case of beer and wrapped sandwiches from the wings*)

PODULLA:

I had to sign three times.

KOZANKA:

What! Sausage and Pilsener for dogs?
(*To* HOD CARRIER)

Say, that's the man from C-Block South.
I thought you were rehearsing?
Rehearsing what? A putsch?

BRENNUS:
The people keep their city clean.

MASON:
Come on, Kozanka, have a beer. Drink.

PLASTERER:
Look at that parasite.

KOZANKA:
They're Western agents, all right.
You can tell by their provocative haircuts.

MASON:
And you're a traitor to the working class.

KOZANKA:
I am the voice of the Workers' and Peasants' State.
If you're against it, you're against the workers.

BRENNUS, COCTOR, *and* VARRO:
The people keep their city clean.
(*The workers take beer, munch sandwiches, and throw the paper in the empty case*)

HOD CARRIER:
Bloodsucking bureaucrats, exploiting
The workers and lining your own pockets.

KOZANKA:
Paid Western agents!

ROAD WORKER:
Bureaucratic swine!

CARPENTER (*tips* KOZANKA *into the case*):
The people keep their city clean! (*Laughter*)

KOZANKA:
Provocateurs and putschists.

ALL:
The people keep their city clean.

KOZANKA:

Class collaborators. Trotskyists.
Lackeys of finance capital.

(*The workers pick up the case with* KOZANKA *in it and carry him off the stage*)

ALL:

The people keep their city clean.

KOZANKA (*offstage, screaming*):

Cosmopolitans! Defeatists!

ALL:

The people keep their city clean!

KOZANKA (*offstage*):

Decadent formalists!
Bourgeois! Corrupted! Westernized . . .

BOSS:

Man, that was a haul! Was the tape running?
The masses will be sent away.
But the recording's here to stay.

(*He sits down by the tape recorder and briefly replays the recorded scenes. The workers come back laughing. Bottles of beer are distributed among them and they drink.* ERWIN *pokes his nose into a pile of books*)

VOLUMNIA (*on her way out to* ERWIN):

He plays. You take refuge in books. The workers drink beer. It's high noon. The revolution is marking time.

CURTAIN

Act III

(The workers are drinking beer. The MECHANIC *is pumping up his bicycle tires, the* MOTORMAN *takes his jacket off the line)*

MOTORMAN:
Any more beer?

HOD CARRIER:
You're drinking too much.

MASON:
It's too quiet around here.

CARPENTER:
And we thought he was our man.

MASON (*to the* PLASTERER):
Remember what you said. All we need is his name. That'll make everybody sit up and take notice.

CARPENTER:
Hell, he hasn't got the same interests.

MASON:
Christ, to think they're shaving Billygoat out there.

CARPENTER:
And we're not with them. What good are we doing around here?

FOREMAN:
I've got my orders: Get his name. — You can do what you like.

CARPENTER:
Are you pigheaded! He's just making monkeys out of us.

MASON:

Maybe they'll turn us in.

FOREMAN:

My orders are: Stick to him until he signs.

MECHANIC:

And suppose it's a flop. — They're only waiting for us in the West.

HOD CARRIER:

We've been in the West. That doesn't count.

CARPENTER:

Out there is what counts.

MASON:

Let's go. Who's with me? (*Pause*)

MOTORMAN:

I just want to see if they haven't lifted my trailer off the tracks. (*Exits*)

FOREMAN (*to the* MASON):

Let him go. You run over to the strike committee.

MECHANIC:

If it's still there.

FOREMAN:

Tell them we're not getting anywhere. Ask them if there's still any point in our hanging around here. Anyway, they'd better send somebody over.

(MASON *and* CARPENTER *exit. A pause*)

ROAD WORKER:

We were cut off one time. In Lapland. Half the company. That's what it feels like today.

FOREMAN (*to* HOD CARRIER):

Do you think the people in Leipzig and Rostock will understand what the trade union man said on the Western radio?

HOD CARRIER:

Man your stations, that's what he said.

PLASTERER:

That ought to get across.

BOSS (*comes in from the right. To the workers*):

Where are my assistants? (*To the* FOREMAN) Taste good? (*To the workers*) I don't know if you're interested, but (*enter* ERWIN) thanks to you, I've seen the light. I've changed the whole scene. Rome. A street. But I'm making the tribunes enter before the plebeians. (*To* ERWIN) Where are Podulla and Litthenner?

ERWIN:

I wouldn't want to upset you. But they've both turned in their scripts for the day.

BOSS:

Litthenner too?

ERWIN:

They announced their decision jointly.

BOSS:

You mean they've gone over to the rebels? I thought we had work to do.

ERWIN (*smiling*):

They're your pupils. My guess is that they're standing in doorways filling their notebooks with useful observations.

BOSS:

Industry wards off temptation.

ERWIN:

And our Egeria is putting on her outdoor make-up.

BOSS:

Does that surprise you? She's always acted blindly, and sometimes to the point.

ERWIN:

Unfortunately . . .

BOSS:

Something else gone wrong?

ERWIN:

I'm sorry. You were in such good form.

BOSS:

Well?

ERWIN:

We've only two plebeians left. Poorly organized as it is, this uprising has a way of pulling you in. — Even I had to hold myself tight.

BOSS:

Let yourself go. One more fool! Answer the call. I can do without a stage manager as long as I've got a single actor on the stage. Get these amateurs out of my theater.

ERWIN (*coolly*):

After all they've done for you.

BOSS:

Be gentle about it.

ERWIN:

Should I give them free tickets?

FOREMAN:

We get it, Boss. We're in the way, we don't know how to act in a theater. — But we want to be in the way. Give us . . .

ROAD WORKER:

That's right. And make it quick.

ERWIN:

Calm down, friends.

ROAD WORKER (*threatening him with his beer bottle*):

Take your paws off me or I'll take a deep breath.

HOD CARRIER:

This is our Wednesday. You can't just stand on the sidelines and watch. You got to pay up. I was only a Socialist, but I paid. With the Nazis— Here, take a look. (*He shows the underside of his forearm*) And if that's how it's got to be, these guys can lock me up again. This is a big day.

FOREMAN:

Something's really happening down there.

PLASTERER:

They're not just yelling about norms.

FOREMAN:

They've whispered long enough: No freedom. Now they're shouting: Freedom.

BOSS:

Shouting ruins the effect.

ROAD WORKER (*tipsy*):

We demand freedom!

ALL THE WORKERS:

Freedom!

ERWIN (*with friendly indulgence*):

Anybody who hears that hollering will think you're asking for breakfast, not freedom.

BOSS:

A good breakfast: that's what they mean by freedom.

MECHANIC:

Well, that's part of it. You can't butter your bread with freedom. When this thing started up, I was against it. Same as you. We should have come out fighting. But before I pick up a loaded gun for lower norms and a pinch of freedom—two years in Russia were enough for me—before yours truly makes a target of himself again, he's clearing out. (*To the workers*)

To old man Adenauer. 'Pon my soul
He ain't no worse than Pieck and Grotewohl.

HOD CARRIER:

Then why are you still here?

MECHANIC:

I'll stay and see how far you get this time.

ROAD WORKER:

My advice is to beat it. They're short on punks over there.

MECHANIC:

But in the West there's pineapple.
Here you can't even find a Christmas candle.
Everything's rationed, even sewing thread.
And it won't get better. (*Takes his bicycle*)

ROAD WORKER:

Over there they'll fatten you up.

HOD CARRIER:

And over there they'll set you in pure gold.

MECHANIC:

And over here? They'll fill me with hot lead.

ROAD WORKER:

Take off his tires, let
Him pedal on his rims. (*Prepares to demolish the bicycle*)

BOSS:

We'll make a note of that. Is the tape running? (ROAD WORKER *desists, thinking the last remark is aimed at him*)
It might have been like this in Rome.
We could have one of the plebeians saying:
I'll stay and see how far you get this time . . .

ERWIN:

Having no bicycle, he'll wear hiking boots . . .

BOSS:

And if it comes to nothing, I'll clear out.

ERWIN:

And if when Coriolanus first appears,
The plebeians threaten: "Then we'll emigrate,"
Why couldn't Coriolanus mock the plebs
By wishing them a rousing "Bon voyage"?

MECHANIC:

And did they emigrate, from Rome, I mean?

BOSS:

They took too long to think it over,
And then some little war broke out,
Pulling a big one in its wake.

FOREMAN:

I don't think that could happen here.

HOD CARRIER:

Are you so sure? (*Consternation. Pause*)

MECHANIC:

Before it breaks out, I'll be gone.

FOREMAN:

Not far, you'll only be in West Berlin.

HOD CARRIER:

Suppose it starts up over there?

PLASTERER:

Hell no. They're sick and tired.

FOREMAN:

Exactly. They won't stir a blessed finger.
The most they'll do—it's free of charge—is set
Up candles in their windows in sympathy.

ROAD WORKER:

I've got a cousin in the Rhineland. All
He cares about is next week's football game.

PLASTERER:

I've got a buddy in Bavaria,
He thinks the country around here's too flat.

HOD CARRIER:

Do you think that anybody knows in Bonn
That Bautzen's prison's badly overcrowded?

FOREMAN:

The people who on Wednesday wrote us off
Proclaim on Sunday: Stand fast, our hearts are with you.

PLASTERER:

If we were Catholics, maybe. But as it is?

MECHANIC:

I'll send you packages from over there.

BOSS:

As Coriolanus says: "Bon voyage."

(*The* MECHANIC *goes out with his bicycle*)

HOD CARRIER (*to the* BOSS):

You could put him in your notebook.

BOSS:

There's room for more.

HOD CARRIER:

But is there room enough?

(ERWIN *goes to the tape recorder and turns it off*)

ROAD WORKER:

Why waste your breath on that guy? All he does
Is stand and watch. He'll never stick his neck out.

HOD CARRIER:

I once knew a horse trader. When he examined a horse's teeth, he looked like you. But we're not horses.

ROAD WORKER:

Or guinea pigs.

FOREMAN:

Doesn't your conscience bother you?

HOD CARRIER:

I know, you get paid: today for yesterday and tomorrow for today. Suppose we paid you? (*He takes out his wallet*) What would you charge us for a consultation?

BOSS (*facing the workers*):

That's how guilt is cooked: You take a sprig of ignorance, a level tablespoonful of misguided passion for freedom, you fold in my knowledgeable hesitation, and there they come, pointing an accusing finger at me: the cook.
(*He turns away and goes to the table*)
What a lousy date this is for the history books. Ah, Livy,

Plutarch, Lenin. If I could only swim with the stream, leave Rome, move, be moved, make statements, true or false, shout; if I could only be beside myself, but in the swim. (*Sits down exhausted*) I'd like to be reading Horace. What do pines look like in the morning?

(*He sits hunched up behind the director's desk*) (WIEBE *and* DAMASCHKE *come in from the left rear. They are both wearing leather jackets and motorcycle goggles pushed up over their foreheads*)

WIEBE:

We've been sent by the strike committee.

ERWIN:

We've had enough delegations.

DAMASCHKE:

We hear you're short on solidarity around here.

ERWIN:

No, not at all. Your cause is ours. Definitely.

WIEBE:

So this, I take it, is the Boss,
The friend of the downtrodden workers?

ERWIN:

Please, can't you see that he's exhausted?

WIEBE:

Exhausted, hell! We need his voice.
Hey, Boss! Hey, comrades! My name's Wiebe.
This is Damaschke. We are delegates
From the districts of Bitterfeld and Merseburg.
The Leuna works and Buna are on strike.
My friend Damaschke of the Electrocombine
And I, Fritz Wiebe, bring you greetings from Halle:
Not just Berlin, the whole Republic
Is sick of Ulbricht, Grotewohl, and Pieck.

(*Exchange of greetings with the workers*)

FOREMAN:

How is it going in Leipzig?

DAMASCHKE:

We're on top.

HOD CARRIER:

In Magdeburg?

DAMASCHKE:

We've cracked the prison.

WIEBE:

And here? You getting anywhere with him?

(*All look toward the* BOSS)

BOSS:

They always have to come in twos, each the other's witness.

ERWIN:

When Paradise was liquidated, how many archangels came to do the job?

BOSS (*stands up. With surprising affability*):

Damaschke, Wiebe? What delightful names!
Rather like Rosencrantz and Guildenstern.
I'm at your service. What is it you need?

(*He bows*)

WIEBE:

In any case not your sarcasm. All right, tell him.

DAMASCHKE:

A strike call. You'd know how to write it.
Maybe an open, a very open letter.

WIEBE:

Don't say maybe.

DAMASCHKE:

You'll think of something.

BOSS:

Good. Who'll take it down?

ERWIN:

You mean it?

BOSS:

I mean it. My contribution:

(ERWIN *sits down beside the* BOSS *with a pad*)

To Ulbricht: whom the people mostly
Call Billygoat. Colon. Comrade Secretary,
No bloodshed. Kindly tell your soldiers that
A carnival is not worth shooting at.
Our citizens are only trying to see
Whether in an emergency our streets
Are wide enough to hold a revolution.
Then like good children they'll go home to mother
And eat potato pancakes for their supper.
But this much, comrade, should be evident,
Our streets and squares are more than adequate
For a rebellion that will end your state.

(*He takes the pad*)

I'll sign. And add a word in my own hand:
And if this people doesn't suit you, comrade,
Find one that suits you better, comrade.

(*He hands* DAMASCHKE *the letter*)

DAMASCHKE:

Hm. You could take this in one way . . . or you could take it in another way.

WIEBE (*tears the letter out of his hand*):

Wisecracks!

ROAD WORKER:

At our expense. Carnival, he says. Hold me before I bust.

BOSS:

They can't read.

WIEBE:

It's irony. It stinks. (*He crumples up the letter and throws it away.* ERWIN *picks it up, smooths it out, and puts it in his pocket*)

BOSS:

All the same, I'm offering a solution that ought to be submitted to our government.

ROAD WORKER:

Submit it yourself.

WIEBE:

For his money the uprising is over. In Leipzig the archives are burning, in Halle they're hanging spies, in Merseburg the bureaucrats are on trial.

ROAD WORKER (*seizing the* BOSS *by the lapels*):

Come on, let's give him the works.

DAMASCHKE:

This one's no better—come along, pal. (*Grabs* ERWIN)

WIEBE:

Do you and I believe in the same Germany, Boss?

BOSS:

Both of us like boiled potatoes.

WIEBE:

Potatoes, Germany: that's two different words.

BOSS:

I eat the one word every day; the other
Devours me every day of my life.

ROAD WORKER:

Just wait. In half a second he'll be rhyming
Potato soup with "Deutschland über Alles."

DAMASCHKE (*shouts indignantly at the* BOSS):

But Germany's divided.

ERWIN:

Spuds and all.

BOSS:

If I remember—and I remember well—
United, it was always pretty messy.

WIEBE:

See, poke them in the right place and they squeal.
I call it treason.

ROAD WORKER:

He's a saboteur.

PLASTERER:

But now he's shown his colors.

WIEBE:

They're traitors. String 'em up. Short shrift!

ROAD WORKER (*looking upward*):

Hang 'em in the middle of their phony Rome!

WIEBE:

In the name of the people.

HOD CARRIER:

Hold it, comrade. Maybe you go in for lynch law in Bitterfeld, but . . .

WIEBE:

In the name of the people . . .

HOD CARRIER:

We're against such methods.

WIEBE:

Any more objections? (*No answer*) That settles it. (*To the* PLASTERER) You get us the equipment. Quick!

PLASTERER:

That won't be so easy. (*Exits right*)

ROAD WORKER (*to the* FOREMAN):

Hold this guy.

(*He hands* ERWIN *to the* FOREMAN, *takes down the clothesline, cuts it and ties two nooses. The spotbar is slowly lowered*)

ERWIN:

We should have ordered native beer. That imported stuff is too strong.

BOSS:

I've always detested this brand of dramatics.

ERWIN:

That's funny. I thought you wanted the revolution to walk on the grass.

ROAD WORKER:

Hold it. — And now we'll take the neck measurements. (*He fastens the nooses to the pipe. He and* WIEBE *put the nooses around the necks of the* BOSS *and* ERWIN)

ERWIN:

But before we have the pleasure of participating in this accelerated dénouement, we hope you'll grant us a few last words.

WIEBE:

Overruled!

DAMASCHKE:

Exception!

WIEBE:

Okay, but keep those neckties on.

ERWIN (*to the* BOSS):

If I could only be Menenius.
What an old fool I am. Suddenly
Stricken with yellow shivers. You speak, Boss.

BOSS:

I've got the hiccups, boy. It's up to you.

ERWIN (*with beads of sweat on his forehead*):

Ye holy demagogues, come help me now!
Even if we must hang, you're in the right.
You hate the bigshots—so you call *us* traitors.
The bigshots ought to hang. So you hang us.
We are the state, is that it? We're the state,
Good. Settle our account, and draw a line.
But before we—the state, that is—are hoisted,
You can afford two pennies' worth of justice:
Putrid as this state is, and stink it does,

We've got no other, the rulers up on top—
Ourselves, that is—we work, incompetently
Perhaps, for you and you. We do our best.
What gripes you—norms and shortages,
Dictatorship—is not the fault of our
Bigshots alone. The bosses across the Rhine
Won't give us time to breathe or turn around.
When we're at odds, they are united against us.

DAMASCHKE:

We've had that music in our soup each day
Instead of noodles. It doesn't make us fat.

ROAD WORKER:

But you get fat, you bosses . . .

FOREMAN:

while we slave.

WIEBE:

So string them up . . .

ROAD WORKER:

and let them dangle
Like jumpingjacks with tonsillitis.

ERWIN:

Before you take the law into your hands,
I'd like—that is, the state would like—to tell you
A story borrowed from our Roman play
But applicable to the world today.

ROAD WORKER:

How do you feel about it?

WIEBE:

Parables!
We've had our bellies full of them in church.
Come on, boys, this is the ascension.

DAMASCHKE:

No, let him talk. Say, look at this contraption.
The boys at home will want to hear the show.

(*He goes to the tape recorder and turns it on*)

WIEBE:

No. I object.

DAMASCHKE:

What's wrong? You scared?

(*Pause*)

ERWIN:

There was a time when all the body's members
Decided, after much too brief discussion,
To thrash the fat round belly with their cudgels,
Because he, so they said, was idle and
Inactive, eating all the meat, while they
Had to bestir themselves like you to meet
The norm, which was set much too high.
The belly answered . . .

PLASTERER:

Go on, I want to hear the belly's story.

ERWIN:

All right, you members, with your sarcastic grins,
Lips curled in mockery . . . Give ear . . .

WIEBE:

Go on. What has he got to say for himself?

ROAD WORKER:

Hear, hear! The asshole with the belly's voice . . .

ERWIN:

He cannot speak until the members are quiet.

ROAD WORKER:

Just make it snappy or I pull the rope.

BOSS:

Ah, how posterity will smile,
When this sound tape is played with our death rattles.
Go on and speak for goodness' sake.

ERWIN:

The belly spoke unhurried, confidently—

For one who has good bowels can be patient:
Well now, my precious members, arms and legs,
Head upon neck, two thumbs, eight fingers—
Where would you be, I pray you, without me?
And the eleventh too would be impotent
To draw the nourishment from celery.
I am the alpha and omega, I'm
The main dispatching station that sends out
Freight trains to your farthest villages.
And what share falls to me? The offal.
You know it, I presume. You all have learned
To wipe yourselves with care. That's all the belly
Gets out of it, apart from worry over
Regular bowel movements, worry whether
You're eating sensibly, you greedy
Unreasonable and insatiable members.
Well, it's the selfsame story with the state.

ROAD WORKER:
The state? How so?

PLASTERER:
The belly is the state.

ERWIN:
The same as we're the state. Myself and him.
What do you know about these things? You big
Toe, with, I bet you, only half a nail.

ROAD WORKER:
Who's a toe? Me? — Say, that's a fact:
One time when I was working on the road,
I broke my left big toe and spent four weeks
In bed. (*Laughter*)

ERWIN:
What did I tell you? Poor big toe!
Important, yes, and hard to do without,
But no perspective, no horizon, wrapped
In socks and bedroom slippers. But does that

Keep you from taking the first step, from shouting:
Let's hang the belly, string the belly up.

PLASTERER:

Which would amount to . . .

ERWIN:

Hanging all the members with the belly.

(*Pause*)

PLASTERER:

I don't want to be hanged.

FOREMAN:

Neither does anybody else.

(*Pause*)

ROAD WORKER:

If you look at it that way . . .

HOD CARRIER:

Give him a hand.

WIEBE:

Who's giving orders around here?

HOD CARRIER:

I am.

ERWIN:

Thanks. Okay, I'm all right.

(*The* ROAD WORKER *helps the* BOSS, *the* FOREMAN *helps* ERWIN *remove the nooses*)

FOREMAN (*while helping* ERWIN):

I was against those methods all along.

(*The* BOSS *looks around on the director's desk, motions the* FOREMAN *to come closer, and gives him back his sheet of paper. The* BOSS *begins to button his coat. A pause.*)

ERWIN (*to the* BOSS):

Well, has the fable about the body's members
Rebelling against the belly convinced you?
It's nonsense hallowed by tradition,

Preserved like corpses in formaldehyde.
The barbs of progress cannot pierce its hide.
(*To the workers*)

My suggestion is that you all trot along home.

(*Pause*)

ROAD WORKER:
It's still raining out.

PLASTERER:
Raining. He means . . . Well, you know what he means.

(*Noise from outside*)

WIEBE:
He's turned you into a bunch of yellowbellies.

(*The noise increases*) Quiet! They're coming.

DAMASCHKE:
We just dropped in here for a friendly visit, see?

(*During the last sentences the* BOSS *has packed up his books and taken his cap. He is about to leave by the rear.* ERWIN *is following him. They are stopped in the middle of the stage*)

WELDER (*rushes in*):
You got some bandage? Quick.

(*The* HAIRDRESSER, *the* WELDER, *and the* RAILROAD WORKER *enter from the left rear. They are dragging the* MASON, *who is carrying a flag*)

RAILROAD WORKER:
Here he is!

ROAD WORKER:
What?

DAMASCHKE:
Who?

FOREMAN:
Man, it's Karl!

HAIRDRESSER:
The medicine chest.

FOREMAN:
Where do you keep it?

ERWIN (*worried, softly to the* BOSS):
You really ought to be going home.

(*The* BOSS *stops still, fascinated. The* MASON *with the flag wrenches himself free*)

MASON:
Never mind the blood. I got it. (*To the* BOSS)
And what have you? I got it . . .

HAIRDRESSER (*to the* BOSS):
From off the top of Brandenburg Arch . . . (*Looks upward, stops*)

WELDER:
All by himself he . . .

HAIRDRESSER (*with wonderment*):
A theater! So this is what it's like! These are
The footlights (*directly to the audience*) and there, that's where the people sit.

MASON:
I took it down myself. And what did you?

HAIRDRESSER (*to the* BOSS):
Just touch him, he's a hero, a hero dripping wet.
He climbed. He took . . .

RAILROAD WORKER:
Let him tell.

HAIRDRESSER:
No, let me tell it over the footlights.

RAILROAD WORKER:
Let him. She's nuts.

MASON:
I was up there, I don't know how I got there,
And you, the crowd below, all shouting: Hurry

Hurry, or you'll never make it—
The Adlon roof is Vopo-blue.

WIEBE:
When we in Halle cracked the city jail
And over in Bitterfeld the boys . . .

HAIRDRESSER:
No, let him talk, you'll tell us later.

DAMASCHKE:
When the committee met in Merseburg
Around a table, where the bosses just . . .
I was elected. Well, I didn't wait.
Comrades, I said. Comrades.

HAIRDRESSER:
So up he went.

MASON:
When once I make my mind up, well.
Franz wanted to come too, because he doesn't
Get dizzy. But I was first to climb
The stairs and ladders that are there
Because the arch was smashed up in the war
And they're supposed to . . .

RAILROAD WORKER:
So arm in arm and ear to ear, we.

HAIRDRESSER:
The Vopos are afraid and beating people.

WELDER:
The boys from Oberspree in trucks . . .

HAIRDRESSER:
But our girls are stabbing back with their umbrellas.

RAILROAD WORKER:
On the way here I saw Vopos.
Throwing their belts away.

WIEBE:
In our plant we opened up the safe,
Man, what a list of names we found!

MASON:

Nothing but wind and rain.
No covering fire.

HAIRDRESSER:

He's sopping wet, my hero.

WELDER:

Never mind that.
Let him go on.

MASON:

So then I crawled
Maybe ten, fifteen feet to the flagpole.
The Vopos on the Adlon roof. So Franz
Hung back at first. But all Berlin
Was down below with cameras . . .
So I . . .

HAIRDRESSER:

He's bleeding again. His bandage is soaked through.

ERWIN (*to the* BOSS):

You ought to take it easy. It's your duty.

BOSS:

You'd better see about some bandage. (ERWIN *exits*)

WIEBE (*to the* BOSS):

And on that list in Bitterfeld
We found the name of every single stool pigeon.

(*The* BOSS *goes toward his armchair.* DAMASCHKE *follows him*)

DAMASCHKE:

Then we debated back and forth. Whether
The Constitution guaranteed the right
To strike. And someone ran to get a copy.

HAIRDRESSER:

He's going to faint. Do something.

WELDER (*gives the* MASON *his flask of schnaps*):

Drink.

MASON (*drinks*):

Okay, I thought. I'll make it quick. But Franz
Was scared. And the crank stuck, because the wire
Was. Never mind, I thought, 'cause down below
All Berlin. So I heaved. But it was slippery.
I damn near fell, kerplop. I heaved again.

HAIRDRESSER:

He pulled so hard he hung in mid-air, both legs
Dangling. He flailed about. And pulled the rope.

MASON:

Slowly. It hardly moved. Because. It wasn't
More than a couple of minutes. Seemed like years.
(*Drinks*)

(*Spellbound, the* BOSS *sits down*)

WELDER:

Then came the crowd from Henningsdorf. Twenty thousand.

MASON:

I wouldn't let it go.

HAIRDRESSER:

Come down, we yelled.

MASON:

I pulled again, brought my full weight to bear.
But then I had to rest. My breath gave out,
And on the Adlon a machine gun.

WELDER:

Take cover, I yelled. Take cover.

(*The* CARPENTER *and the* MACHINIST *enter left rear*)

CARPENTER:

Well, you get your reading matter?

MACHINIST:

The boys from Beeskow can't get through.

FOREMAN:

And the Treptow Electric Works?

CARPENTER:

Nine thousand on the road.

HOD CARRIER:

And Plania? And the Abus Machine Works?

MACHINIST:

They're on their way. But the rain keeps coming down.

CARPENTER:

The newspaper stands won't burn.

MACHINIST:

Our people went into the Trade Commission. It was dry in there.

ROAD WORKER:

Same here. Nice dry theater. We wanted a written statement, but all we got was beer.

FOREMAN:

There's still some left. (*Passes a bottle to the* CARPENTER *and the* MACHINIST)

HAIRDRESSER:

What's wrong with you guys? He comes first, 'cause he's
(*Grabs the bottle, gives it to the* MASON)
A hero. If he hadn't kept on pulling . . .
(*Shows the workers the flag*)
That flag would still be up there on its pole.

MASON:

Franz didn't dare. I did it with my knife.
When it was down, he came up from below.
I was all in. My head was spinning. Franz
Went down and took it off the ledge . . .
(*Imitates a machine gun*)
Rat-tat-tat-tat, I'm telling you. We two
Flat on our faces. Heels down. Holding
On to that flag for dear life.
I get a good grip. Double or quits. And rolled
Out of the line of fire.

(RUFUS *and* FLAVUS, *no longer in costume, come in from the street*)

FLAVUS:

We hear they're coming in from Jüterbog. Two columns.

RUFUS:

Boss, they say the Soviets are warming up their tanks in Döberitz.

CARPENTER:

Let them come. You should see the crowd in Spittelmarkt, in Alexanderplatz. You couldn't drop a pin between them. (*Inarticulate loudspeaker noises are heard from the distance*)

FLAVUS:

Except they don't know where to go. They run from Potsdamer Platz to Alexanderplatz and from there to Marx-Engels-Platz

RUFUS:

. . . and the people from Strausberger Platz were already on their way to the government quarter . . .

FLAVUS:

. . . where the people from Spittelmarkt had just been before going to Marx-Engels-Platz . . .

RUFUS:

where they split up because they thought the crowd from Potsdamer Platz was going to Marx-Engels-Platz . . .

FLAVUS:

And the people from Strausberger Platz had already started for the government quarter.

RUFUS:

. . . where the people from Spittelmarkt had just been.

ERWIN (*enters with bandages*):

They're blocking off Friedrichstrasse.

KOZANKA'S VOICE (*over the loudspeaker in the distance*):

Comrades, you are being addressed by National Prize

Winner Kozanka! Masons, railroad men, progressive workers! (*Louder*) Agents of the West, provocateurs, putschists!

(*During* KOZANKA'S *speech workers' choruses in the distance*):

"All the traffic lights are green,
When workers protest in the rain."
"The Vopo cops are good and mad,
Because the rain don't make us sad."
"Not Grotewohl or Adenauer,
But unified with Ollenhauer."

ERWIN:

The government is sending fire hoses and loudspeaker cars. (*Gives the* HAIRDRESSER *the bandage. She begins to bandage the* MASON)

KOZANKA'S VOICE:

Agitators, revanchists, fascists!

CARPENTER:

We shut him up a little while ago.

WIEBE:

Let him holler. Rostock is with us. So are Magdeburg and Görlitz. We demand the immediate dissolution.

KOZANKA'S VOICE:

Unmask the Western agents . . .

WIEBE:

We demand the resignation of the so-called . . .

KOZANKA'S VOICE:

At the last Party Congress . . .

WIEBE:

The formation of a new . . .

KOZANKA'S VOICE:

But, we, shoulder to shoulder with the glorious . . .

WIEBE:

All-German . . .

KOZANKA'S VOICE:

But the class enemies in the West.

WIEBE:

And demand the legalization of all . . .

KOZANKA'S VOICE:

Because the Soviet power . . .

DAMASCHKE:

Free, secret, and direct . . .

WIEBE:

Elections! We demand elections!

KOZANKA'S VOICE:

Errors, yes, but that cannot justify. The progressive peace-loving camp.

WIEBE:

We furthermore demand the immediate elimination. And the release . . .

DAMASCHKE:

Of all political prisoners.

KOZANKA:

But the tools of the capitalist warmongers.

DAMASCHKE:

On religious and political grounds no one.

KOZANKA'S VOICE:

But the provocateurs and putschists.

WIEBE:

And demand freedom.

KOZANKA'S VOICE:

Will not escape the punishment they.

WIEBE:

Freedom!

HAIRDRESSER:

Quiet, comrades! (*Pause. The sound of tanks in the distance*)

Listen, pounding the cobbles in
The distance. Tanks.

DAMASCHKE:

If that's the ticket,
It means we're sunk.

PLASTERER (*after a short pause, half to himself*):
I bet it's just her nerves.

CARPENTER:

She hears
The raindrops beating on the roofs.

DAMASCHKE:
In all my life I never hurt a fly.
He yes. But I've done hardly anything.
I haven't anything to hide. No, nothing!
I'll tell them which of us.
(*Runs out*)
Don't shoot. Don't fire on Germans!

WIEBE (*after a pause, to the workers*):
His name is Hans Damaschke. Don't forget it.

(*He looks from one to the other. No one reacts. The sound of tanks grows louder. Suddenly he turns and leaves*)

HAIRDRESSER:
Oh, who will mourn with me? And whom
Shall I accuse? The radiant body of freedom
Plugged full of lead? And no one, only you . . .

MASON (*paying no attention to her*):
And so I held it up. And then I let
It drop into the street. Kerplunk.

HAIRDRESSER:
Come down, all Berlin cried. Come down.

MASON:
And that was when I got it in the shin.

HAIRDRESSER:
They hoisted him upon their shoulders. Franz too.

MASON:

And someone in the crowd gave me his watch. (*Shows the watch*)

HAIRDRESSER (*picking up the flag*):

They wanted to tear the flag. But I said no.
And others took out lighters in the rain.
But when it wouldn't burn, he took it, he,
Because, it's his, because he, his and no one
Else's, and wound it three times round his body.
He marched round in a circle. Cameras snapped him
A hundred times, the hero, hero, hero!

HOD CARRIER:

But supposing those are really tanks?

HAIRDRESSER:

Come out and see the big fat toads that clank
Their iron entrails down our streets.

ROAD WORKER:

There's nothing you can do. You can only look.

HAIRDRESSER:

You cowards. Can't you think of anything?

ERWIN:

She could have been written by you, Boss.

BOSS:

I'm afraid
She was.

HAIRDRESSER:

You're not ashamed? Why, I
Could cripple one of those things with a hairpin.

BOSS:

This little soprano trumpet wakens dreams
That should be better left to sleep.

HAIRDRESSER:

I know you well.

BOSS:

And you're not strange to me.

HAIRDRESSER:

I've been a hairdresser four years now,
But I went to the theater when I was seventeen.
That's where I sat when Katrin, mute
Katrin, sat drumming on the roof.
As now I scream. The tanks are coming!
Come on, Boss. Come, and crawl out of that shell:
And we'll put on a play for the whole world,
Enacted in the street, on barricades.
Molotov cocktails. Plaster in exhaust pipes.
Their sight slits plugged until they zigzag
Blindly and clash. They'll all be turned to scrap
If you and I, the two of us,
Just give Berlin the sign. Come on!

BOSS (*laughing*):

Should I? You want?

HAIRDRESSER:

Yes, come, the two of us.

BOSS (*still laughing*):

We two?

HAIRDRESSER:

You, I, and all of us. Come on.

BOSS:

What do you think? Me? In the midst, unchained . . . ?

HAIRDRESSER:

Down the Linden, to Marx-Engels-Platz . . .

BOSS:

As in my youth, under a sky swept clean . . .

HAIRDRESSER:

We'll take the radio station and you'll speak!

BOSS:

Alone for the time of a poem. Flight . . .

HAIRDRESSER:

Speak to the world.

BOSS:

Conjure up chaos, rivers . . .

HAIRDRESSER:

Then come.

BOSS:

Right now?

HAIRDRESSER:

Yes, now.

BOSS:

I'm coming.

(*The* HAIRDRESSER *in the lead, the* BOSS *follows. The workers,* FLAVUS, RUFUS, *and* ERWIN *are about to join in.* VOLUMNIA *comes toward them*)

VOLUMNIA:

Whose funeral have you been invited to? (*To* ERWIN) Who gets buried in the late afternoon?

ERWIN:

Stalin, I presume. His kind have seven lives.

VOLUMNIA:

Eight if you ask me. (*To the* BOSS) He is arisen and now he's celebrating Easter.

HAIRDRESSER:

Don't listen. Throw your ears away.

VOLUMNIA (*shows a leaflet*):

Here, signed Dibrova, City Commandant. All right, throw it away, but don't pretend to be blind.

PLASTERER (*reads*):

State of emergency. Martial law.

VOLUMNIA:

Just calm down, and start thinking up the answers. Because there are going to be questions. (*The* BOSS *takes the flag from the* HAIRDRESSER)

HAIRDRESSER (*to the* BOSS):

That was a short engagement.

(VOLUMNIA *and* ERWIN *escort the* HAIRDRESSER *and the workers off the stage*)

VOLUMNIA:

We'll take the stage exit. You go through the storeroom.

(VOLUMNIA *and* ERWIN *exit in opposite directions, each with a group*)

ERWIN:

And don't stick together. Go by twos and threes. (*All go out. The* BOSS *remains alone, holding the flag*)

BOSS:

Benighted children worshiping a dove:
"Come, Holy Spirit; come abide with us."
Come, come, my dove, oh come sweet reason.
Come, Holy Spirit, thou the first atheist.
Don't mind the stairs, take the emergency
Door, and assail me with relentless hardware.
I, knowing, wily, cool-headed and alone,
Was almost with them for the time it takes
To breathe a poem. Now I'm left behind.
And empty bottles stare at me as if
They saw into my soul. And this red rag has
Been thrust upon me like an orphan babe.
What can I do with it? Whom should I dress
In it? Coriolanus? This rubbish blocked
My way, I stumbled and I went no further.
And these ten fingers, ten, twice five, are turned
To heavy gold with hesitation.
Here stood a mason, class of '22:
"He's writing something there. Is that for us?"
And there the old Socialist:
"This is our Wednesday, Boss."
What did I say? It doesn't touch me.
The Holy Spirit breathed, and I mistook

It for a draft, and cried:
Who's come here to molest me?

(*He goes to the tape recorder. After a glance at a file card, he lets the tape run audibly backward*)

CURTAIN

Act IV

(The BOSS *is still sitting by the tape recorder. The tape is running: "Somebody's got to tell him. Do you know what you are? Give it to him good. You, you, you're a rotten, no-good, slimy, underhanded . . . you, you . . . I tell you, you're a . . ." The* BOSS *stops the tape.* ERWIN *comes in slowly from the rear. He stops in the middle of the stage)*

BOSS *(after a pause)*:
Well?

ERWIN:
The people are all afraid to sneeze.

BOSS:
But how do they feel? Dejected?

ERWIN:
Don't ask. It makes All Souls look like Mardi Gras.

BOSS:
So they've started making arrests?

ERWIN:
It takes a little while to draw up lists. Remember? (LITTHENNER *and* PODULLA *come in from the street, out of breath)*

PODULLA *(provocatively)*:
What material! Enough for three plays and an adaptation. You were dead right, Boss. Your theory has been confirmed. All we have to do is work, rehearse, modify, and above all preserve our God-damned serenity.

LITTHENNER:

People have been killed, Boss.

PODULLA:

Incidentals! Let's start digesting this new material: Can tanks be used on the stage? What do you think, Boss?

LITTHENNER:

They were Soviet tanks.

PODULLA (*cynically*):

Why, so they were. The question is: Can we have a scene—or maybe even a whole play—taking place in a cross-section of a Soviet tank? (*Begins setting up chairs in such a way as to indicate a tank*)

LITTHENNER:

They sent our workers scurrying.

ERWIN:

If you ask me, we'd better be thinking that it's going to be our turn next.

LITTHENNER:

Have they passed any resolutions?

ERWIN:

They're still in session.

(COCTOR, VARRO, *and* BRENNUS*—no longer in costume—come in from the street*)

COCTOR:

Boss! It wasn't like we thought. They sawed off the aerials. I saw masons stuffing plaster in the sight slits.

BRENNUS:

One of them, I saw him, rolled up his briefcase and jammed it into the exhaust pipe.

PODULLA:

Exactly: we could show a tank being taken apart on the stage. (*Busies himself with his chairs*)

VARRO:

They tried it with crowbars and T-girders.

BRENNUS:

One man was running back and forth like crazy in front of that tank, then up he goes like a monkey, yelling: Watch out, comrades, I'm going to explode.

VARRO:

He was pretty flat after the column had . . .

LITTHENNER:

But the Russians didn't know why or where they . . .

PODULLA:

Tank Commander to Tovarich Tank Driver: Do you see any Amerikanski tanks?

LITTHENNER:

They were circling around on Unter den Linden and Alexanderplatz.

PODULLA:

Tank Driver to Tovarich Commander: All I can see is progressive workers on bicycles. Looking for Amerikanski tanks same as us.

LITTHENNER:

Pull yourself together.

PODULLA:

Commander to Tovarich Radio Operator: Contact General Dibrova, the City Commandant. Ask him where and what we.

ERWIN (*shouting*):

Stop it!

PODULLA:

Radio Operator to Commander: Unable to contact Tovarich General.

ERWIN (*softly*):

Stop it, I tell you! (*Silence*)

All I could see was tanks. And our own helplessness.

BRENNUS:

The tanks were circling like mad.

LITTHENNER:

I saw the tanks. And I saw him.

PODULLA:

I had only my bare hands. But I had to do something.

LITTHENNER:

He picked up stones and threw them. Some were hits.

PODULLA:

It made me feel better. Throwing stones.

(KOZANKA *and* VOLUMNIA *enter*)

KOZANKA:

Still working hard? Developed some new, world-shattering theories? What do you say, Boss? Why so quiet? Run out of jokes? And our little artist friends? Sweating through their make-up? — Well, here I am. Your star performer asked me to come: Come, Kozanka, come. We need your advice. Let's get together and. All right if I occupy the throne? (*He sits down in the director's chair.* VOLUMNIA *approaches the* BOSS. ERWIN *follows*)

VOLUMNIA:

You're surprised that I've soiled my fingers?

BOSS:

Your spirit of self-sacrifice is for the birds.

VOLUMNIA:

Think of your theater. This is a new situation. We have to react.

BOSS:

Never mind that plural. I didn't tell you to go crawling.

ERWIN:

We mustn't give them the impression that anyone in this house hesitated—for so much as a second.

KOZANKA:

Are you done talking?

VOLUMNIA:

Why don't you ask him to contribute something? He's written plays.

BOSS:

There are limits to my guile.

KOZANKA (*who has been scrutinizing the plebeians and assistants*):

I know that face. And this one, and those two. I made a mental note. In with the mob. Am I right? — Well, there you have it.

BOSS (*grasps the situation, approaches* KOZANKA *with affability*):

I've heard about your speeches. Big success, I hear.

KOZANKA:

Yes. I spoke.

BOSS:

Off the cuff? I couldn't have done that.

KOZANKA:

Of course not. Whom would you speak to? They didn't say boo. (*To the plebeians and assistants*) Did you? . . . When I addressed you from the top of that . . .

BOSS:

But you had a mike?

KOZANKA:

No mike.
On the tank without a mike:
Hear me, ye masons, yea verily!
Gratis, for free, overwhelming the people with
Gifts, the bright socialist sun shone down on you.
Nevertheless you have made common
Cause with unscrupulous elements sold out to the West,
Pimps, contemptible riffraff, teen-age delinquents.

PODULLA (*with affected seriousness*):

Provocateurs and fascist agents . . .

KOZANKA:

Putschists, revanchists, reactionaries!
Mildly the Vopos averted their eyes,

Squeezing no triggers, unrolling no hoses,
Judging that this was brief folly, that you must be
Temporarily out of your senses to
Follow an agent, who called himself carpenter.
Carpenter, ha! That man was a maker of coffins. But
As with the flat of the hand a fastidious citizen
Brushes the dust off his jacket, the glorious
Soviet Army swept clean our socialist city.

BOSS (*as though to himself*):

Yes, I know, some were killed.

KOZANKA:

Therefore, inclined to indulgence, I say: You were
Wise not to battle with comrades. For war presupposes a
Reason, and reason, my friends, you had none. And
Now like obedient children you'd all better trundle
Off to your pillows before the belfry strikes nine. But
When the sun rises tomorrow, you'll kindly
Get back to work voluntarily, masons, my friends,
Pouring cement, mixing mortar, and laying
Stone upon stone, voluntarily meeting the
Norms, till your guilt is atoned and your blunder forgotten.

(*Silence*)

BOSS (*applauds briefly*):

What courage, what vigor, Kozanka! Why, you thundered as eloquently and parabolically from the turret of that tank as Christ from the summit of the universe.

KOZANKA:

Your enthusiasm tells me that you will add your name to my list. Would you like me to tell you the names of all the others who have joined me in expressing their unqualified support of the Socialist Unity Party?

BOSS:

Never mind. I know all the big names. I've seen them assembled on paper whenever there was an occasion to demonstrate loyalty.

KOZANKA:

That will make it easy for you to contribute yours, the biggest name of all.

(*He hands the* BOSS *the paper. The* BOSS *takes it but does not look at it. A pause*)

VOLUMNIA (*goes up to the* BOSS *after a glance at* ERWIN):

They'll cancel our new theater. We've been working for months with that revolving stage in mind. And you act as if this were some private quarrel. (*The* BOSS *does not react*) We insist that you dissociate yourself from all counterrevolutionary machinations and congratulate—yes, congratulate—the government on its victory over the putschists and provocateurs. — Want me to sign first? (*The* BOSS *returns the paper to* KOZANKA) Think of us, think of your theater.

BOSS:

What is that animal anyway? What do they call it? The one that changes its color at will? I've got it. A chameleon. Chameleon! No! How often do you think I can change color? First you want me to play the hero; when I wouldn't join the workers in the street, you called me Coriolanus. And now you want me to embrace Kozanka as he embraced Aufidius. What parts you offer me! The trouble is they're too easy to play. — Let *him* sign! (*Shakes the Coriolanus dummy*) See, he's moving.

KOZANKA:

Save your wit. Just sign here.

BOSS:

Even if I wore gloves, my fingers would go on strike.

KOZANKA:

The initials will do. — Is it so difficult?

BOSS (*speaking each word in* KOZANKA'S *face*):

When the masons talked about victory, they struck me as absurd. It took their defeat to convince me . . .

VOLUMNIA:

Watch your step.

KOZANKA (*challenging*):

Of what?

BOSS:

. . . for instance, that we can't change Shakespeare unless we change ourselves.

LITTHENNER:

You mean we're going to drop Coriolanus?

BOSS:

He has dropped us. With contempt. From this day on we'll be at cross-purposes. Where there was solid ground a few hours ago, I see gaping, grinning cracks. Only yesterday I was rich in words of vilification. Today I haven't a single one to fit him, you, or myself. — And to think we wanted to demolish him, the colossus Coriolanus. We ourselves are colossal and deserve to be demolished. (*To the plebeians*) You may go. (*The plebeians exit. To* LITTHENNER *and* PODULLA) Put the scripts away. Put the plebeians' rags in moth balls. Take the Roman sets to the storehouse. — And you, too, Kozanka. This stage has seen too much of you.

(*The* BOSS *goes to the director's desk and sits down. With exaggerated dignity, he puts on his glasses, puts the paper in place, and begins to write*)

PODULLA:

He's dropped the play.

KOZANKA:

Dropped the play? Your shop's going to be closed up. Have I made myself clear?

VOLUMNIA:

Perfectly clear. Liquidate, liquidate. That's all you know how to say.

ERWIN:

Come, come. Every humanist knows how much the theater has done to transform apes into men. And Kozanka is a humanist, is he not?

KOZANKA:

I've nothing against the theater in itself, but . . .

PODULLA (*taking him at his word, with dialectical sharpness*):

We call it the "theater for others," just as the correct term is not the "thing in itself" but the "thing for others."

LITTHENNER (*in support of* PODULLA):

He'd better brush up on his Hegel.

ERWIN:

For Hegel himself regarded Kozanka's "thing in itself" as a truthless abstraction.

KOZANKA:

Nonsense! I did say something about the theater in itself, but . . .

ERWIN:

That, my friend, is to speak with Kant . . .

KOZANKA:

Don't bother me with Kant.

ERWIN:

. . . and to postulate an unknowable theater.

PODULLA:

Unknowable in Kant's and Kozanka's terms.

KOZANKA:

Comrades, I repeat: I spoke of the theater in itself and as such, but . . .

PODULLA:

Because he's incapable of dialectical thinking.

KOZANKA:

I, incapable?! I?

ERWIN:

If instead of talking about the "theater in itself" he had spoken with Lenin of the "theater for others" . . .

PODULLA:

On what basis?

LITTHENNER:

On the basis of the "thing for others," of which Hegel speaks.

ERWIN:

. . . in that case we might have felt that it had something to do with us when he talked about shutting up our shop.

VOLUMNIA:

I never thought he knew the first thing about Marxism.

KOZANKA:

I'll show you what I know. I've got the whole thing at my fingertips.

VOLUMNIA:

He's ignorant. He's incompetent. But what a voice!

KOZANKA:

What do you want me to quote from? The Communist Manifesto? *Das Kapital*? From Three Sources and Three Components? Something from One Step Forward and Two Steps Backward? Do you want: What does it mean during the Revolution . . . or would you rather have: How to promote the . . . Ask me! Ask me! I know them all by heart. Controversial questions. Plekhanov was and remains. Even then there were reformists, class collaborators, and renegades. Just look at the Party's resolution on municipal ownership, at the Stockholm Congress of 1906. Undialectical? Don't make me laugh. Unification of opposites. Negation. The business with the grain of barley. Or how about this? Only in a communist society, when once and for all the resistance of the, when capitalism has. And classes have ceased. Only then can we speak of freedom, only then can there and will there be genuine. And then alone will democracy. Because of the simple and obvious fact. Freedom from capitalist slavery. Fall into the habit of observing the elementary. Preached for thousands. Without violence, without coercion, without the special coercive apparatus known as the state. That's right, *without*! And now your signature. Or else!

(VOLUMNIA *bursts out laughing and can't stop.* LITTHENNER *and* PODULLA *join in the laughter.* KOZANKA *out of breath*)

I fail to see anything funny. (*To* VOLUMNIA) You'll be laughing on the other side of your face before long. This theater's going to be shorthanded. (*Indicates prison bars with his fingers, points to* LITTHENNER, PODULLA) Ever hear of Bautzen? Him. And him. And those two can look forward to a nice long guest performance in Bautzen. (*To the* BOSS) And you're not indispensable either. (*He exits*)

ERWIN (*gravely*):

I'm afraid we've thrown out a boomerang. And who's going to catch it when it comes back?

BOSS:

Kozanka isn't the only one who has trouble expressing himself.

VOLUMNIA:

Have you written an obituary on the uprising? (*To* ERWIN) I was beginning to think he'd forgotten how to write. And then he came up with a creation. (*Takes the paper away from him*)

BOSS:

It's the fourth draft. Too many interruptions.

(VOLUMNIA *and* ERWIN *glance through the text. Then* ERWIN *reads aloud*)

ERWIN:

To the First Secretary of the Central Committee . . .

VOLUMNIA (*takes the paper away from him*):

Why read this pussyfooting document aloud? Three succinct paragraphs. The first two are critical; you say the measures taken by the government, in other words the Party, were premature. In the third and last something makes you proclaim your solidarity with the same people you attacked in the first two. Why not come out for Kozanka in the first place? Because they'll cross out the critical paragraphs and trumpet the solidarity until you die of shame.

BOSS:

Here, underneath the original, I have a copy. Blessed be carbon paper.

ERWIN:

Those things are locked up in the archives; they get published with your posthumous papers when it's too late.

VOLUMNIA:

And legends will grow up. Deep down he was against. Or deep down he was for. That's the way he spoke, but his heart—hm, what about his heart? Everybody will have his own interpretation: cynical opportunist, home-grown idealist; all he really cared about was theater; he wrote and thought for the people. What people? Speak out. Give them a piece of your mind or knuckle under. And dovetail your sentences, don't leave an opening for their scissors.

BOSS:

No one will dare to censor me.

VOLUMNIA:

Don't be childish. You know perfectly well you're going to be cut.

ERWIN:

And even uncut it's feeble. Did you really write this? It's feeble, it's embarrassing.

BOSS:

Like the subject matter. Do you want me to write: I congratulate the meritorious murderers of the people. Or I congratulate the ignorant survivors of a feeble uprising. And what congratulations will reach the dead? — And I, capable of nothing but small, embarrassed words, stood on the sidelines. Masons, railroad workers, welders and cable winders remained alone. Housewives didn't hang back. Even some of the Vopos threw off their belts. They'll be court-martialed. In our camp they'll add new wings to the prisons. — And in the Western camp, too, lies will become official truths. The face of hypocrisy will rehearse a display of mourning. My farseeing eye sees national rags falling to half-mast. I can hear whole platoons of orators sucking the word "freedom" empty. I can see the years hobbling by. And after the fatal calendar leaf has been plucked ten or eleven times, they'll take to celebrating the seventeenth with beer orgies as they celebrated the Battle of Sedan in my childhood. In the West I see a well-fed nation picnicking in the green. What's left? Bottles drained in celebration, sandwich papers, beer corpses and real corpses: for on holidays the traffic takes its meed of corpses. But here, after ten or eleven years, the prisons will vomit up the wreckage of this uprising. Accusation will run rampant, address and mail a thousand packages of guilt. We've got our package already.

(*Hands the original and copy to* LITTHENNER *and* PODULLA)

Kindly play the messengers. The original to the Central Committee; the copy to friends in the West for safekeeping.

PODULLA:

Boss, they'll say we're sitting on the fence.

BOSS:

Answer, what better seat have you to offer?

LITTHENNER:

And history?

BOSS:

Will judge.

PODULLA:

It will convict us.

BOSS:

Not so easily if you deliver this original and this copy.

LITTHENNER:

Won't we feel ashamed of ourselves for the rest of our lives?

BOSS:

I feel ashamed already.

(LITTHENNER *and* PODULLA *exit.* ERWIN *pulls the director's chair close to the* BOSS)

ERWIN:

You ought to sit down.

BOSS:

Your solicitude makes me feel small.

VOLUMNIA:

Solicitude or not—you're going to have insomnia.

ERWIN:

Well, now what? A trip? Something to cheer you up?

BOSS:

I've rented a house on a lake, with poplars around it.

VOLUMNIA:

It will catch up with you all the same.

BOSS:

I could watch the people rowing. Knocking themselves out. Or read Horace again. We can always fall back on books.

VOLUMNIA:

They'll vomit up the reader.

BOSS:

Well, maybe some poems will hatch from all this misery.

VOLUMNIA:

You're going to write again?

BOSS:

Does that frighten you?

VOLUMNIA:

Yes, my dear. I'm afraid the truth will make you eloquent.

BOSS (*stands up, gathers his papers*):

If I could write as I used to. When hardly anything troubled me. Tasted like soft-boiled eggs and helped for a little while. Then later, among the birches in the north, wherever I and my suitcase happened to be, prepared for a quick getaway. Surviving my friends. Taciturn. With fewer and fewer certitudes.

ERWIN:

Wouldn't it be wiser to start a play?

BOSS:

Something new, about current events?

VOLUMNIA:

All right, go to the country. — But leave your guile here. We might need it tomorrow. (*She exits*)

ERWIN:

Would I be in the way if I came out for the weekend? There ought to be enough quiet for two. (*Slowly follows* VOLUMNIA)

(*The* BOSS *packs his papers, takes his cap, and goes slowly to the tape recorder. He stands in front of it.* KOWALSKI, *the electrician, comes in from the wings right, dressed to go home*)

KOWALSKI:

Boss?

BOSS:

Yes, Kowalski, what is it?

KOWALSKI:

I wanted to remind you about my vacation before you.

BOSS:

Take all the vacation you want, Kowalski.

KOWALSKI:

Thank you, Boss. I've installed the new low-frequency machines. (*He crosses the stage and exits left rear. The iron door slams. The* BOSS *looks at the tape recorder*)

BOSS:

Condemned to live forever with voices in my ears. You. You. I'll tell you. Do you know what you are? You, you, you're a . . . You poor babes in the woods! Bowed down with guilt, I accuse you!

(*He exits slowly*)

CURTAIN

The Uprising of June 17, 1953

Documentary Report by Uta Gerhardt

The workers' uprising of June 16 and 17 in East Berlin was touched off by the decision of the East German government to impose a general increase of at least 10 per cent in the work norms (units of work to be produced in a given time) to take effect on June 30. Increases in the norms were nothing new, but up until then they had been "voluntary," that is, the Party delegates and union officials in a given shop would put pressure on the workers, who would then "vote" to increase their productivity. Formally, it was the workers who did the deciding. Now the forms were abandoned. The following resolution was passed by the Central Committee of the Socialist Unity Party and ratified by the Council of Ministers of the German Democratic Republic on May 28:

> In compliance with the decision of the Council of Ministers, the competent ministries and state secretaries will establish guidelines covering the increase in the work norms of each enterprise; the enterprise management in turn will apportion this over-all increase among its various departments. In cooperation with the leadership of the unions involved, the competent ministries and state secretaries will immediately order a general review of the work norms in the enterprises under their control. The enterprise managements will order reviews of the work norms in their enterprises, to be completed by June 3, 1953, in consultation with the union leadership. The new and increased work norms will be based on these reviews and at least equal the guideline in every enterprise. To this end

section heads, technicians, and norm planners will discuss their proposals with activists and experienced workers.[1]

Even the government's campaign for "voluntary" norm increases, carried on through management officials and the press since the Party Congress of July, 1952, had aroused considerable opposition among the workers. There had been isolated strikes. When the decision of May 28 became known, opposition to the directives of the government grew to open protest among a large part of the workers. On June 14, even the Central Organ of the Socialist Unity Party, *Das Neue Deutschland,* in an article titled "Enough of Sledge-hammer Tactics," joined in the protest against the administrative increase of the norms, and reported from the shops:

> On May 28 a conference of brigade leaders and activists was held at VEB [Volkseigener Betrieb—State Industry] headquarters. The purpose of the conference was to discuss and decide upon a general norm increase averaging 10 per cent. And what happened? The majority opposed the general increase. At almost the same time the alarming news arrived from Section G-North of the Stalin-Allee construction project that several carpenter brigades had not resumed work that morning because of differences of opinion with the norm division. On Strausbergerplatz, where VEB carpenter brigades are also employed, similar incidents occurred.[2]

On June 13 in the course of a boat ride organized by VEB Industrial Construction, but in which members from VEB Housing Construction also participated, the norm increase was discussed and the possibility of a strike considered. On Monday, June 15, the workers on several building sites went on strike; they sent a resolution to the President of the Council of Ministers, demanding that the increase be rescinded.

On the morning of June 16, *Die Tribüne,* organ of the government-controlled unions, announced that the decisions of the Central Committee and the Council of Ministers remained unchanged:

[1] *Tägliche Rundschau* (East Berlin), May 30, 1953.
[2] *Neues Deutschland,* June 6, 1953.

These decisions lend the significant mass movement for voluntary norm increases an organized character. They provide for a general survey of the norms in our state enterprises and an average increase of at least 10 per cent, according to the possibilities, effective June 30.[3]

This article was the last straw and provoked an immediate reaction.

There were two reasons on account of which a protest march formed on the morning of June 16 at the building site Block 40 of Stalin-Allee. Its purpose was to submit a demand for a reduction of the norms to the central trade union office and the government.

Otto Lehmann's article, which appeared on the morning of the 16th and was read to the workers by a member of the union shop committee, had raised the construction workers' excitement to a high pitch. After long discussions on the building site they had come to the conclusion that the two delegates, who had been chosen the day before, could not be sent alone to trade union headquarters and the government, because once arrived they might be arrested. It was quickly decided that all must go together. One worker declared that the time for action had come; another called upon all those wishing to participate to step out to the right. And, as one construction worker later remarked: "The whole crowd went over to the right." A few minutes later three hundred construction workers from Block 40 were under way. They carried a placard saying: "We demand reduction of the norms."

The workers from the hospital site in Friedrichshain had meanwhile decided to accompany their delegation to the president to lend greater force to their demands.

From the start the construction workers lacked leadership, for no strike committees had been chosen on the two construction sites. Consequently chance was to play a large part in the development of the demonstration.

The workers from Block 40 and the Friedrichshain construction site first marched to other construction sites on Stalin-Allee and vicinity to enlist their comrades in the demonstration. Then the marchers, considerably swelled in number, started for FDGB [Trade Union] headquarters on Wallstrasse.

[3] *Die Tribüne*, June 16, 1953.

At this point the purpose of the march was definitely limited to a protest against the norm increase.

When the workers found the building closed up tight and no one came out to negotiate with them, the steadily growing procession started for the Ministry building on Leipziger Strasse. It had meanwhile been joined by workers from the Import and Export Building construction site, the Lindenstrasse housing development, the Opera construction site, and other shops. An estimated ten thousand gathered outside the Ministry building. Here too everything was closed, and at first no one seemed willing to negotiate with the workers. Tempers mounted.

After some time Secretary of State Walther, a woman, came out. She was mistaken for Ulbricht's secretary, and therefore shouted down by the demonstrators, who wanted Ulbricht himself. Minister Selbmann (the only top official of the SUP in the building who had the courage to face the workers) was also booed and prevented from speaking. To quote one of the demonstrators: "Next an official climbed the platform and introduced himself as Professor Havemann." It is said that he began a lecture on the economic foundations and anomalies of their present situation. "We didn't trust him. There was more and more noise. We booed him down too." . . .

Some of the workers realized that the government had been caught off its guard and that this weakness should be exploited, that it was time to go beyond the limited question of norms and raise more sweeping, political demands. A few speakers actually did formulate political aims and were wildly applauded by the crowd. But for want of leadership, the enthusiasm gradually died down.

When, for instance, at about two o'clock, Selbmann, trying for a second time, managed to make himself heard and announced that the Council of Ministers had withdrawn the administrative increase in the norms, because it had been a mistake, a construction worker pushed him aside, saying that there was more to the matter than norms, that the government should take the consequences of its mistakes and resign.

But it was significant for the situation, for the uncertainty and lack of leadership in the demonstration, that nothing further happened. After the enthusiastic cheering of the others had ebbed away, no new speaker followed up; again, uncertainty spread among the workers.

Later another worker climbed up on the table and called for a general strike unless the government resigned. There was no point in waiting any longer, he said. If Grotewohl and Ulbricht were not showing themselves within the next half hour, the workers should march off and proclaim a general strike. This was greeted by more applause. But without organization and leadership no concerted action was possible. After only five minutes more, the workers started back to their work sites, to Stalin-Allee.[4]

In the course of the afternoon, the demonstrators proclaimed a general strike from a loudspeaker truck they had appropriated; a worker manned it spontaneously and kept calling on all the workers of Berlin to rally on Strausbergerplatz on the morning of June 17.

In the early morning of the following day a voice in West Berlin spoke in behalf of the demonstrators. In the afternoon of the 16th a group of workers had gone to RIAS [Radio in the American Sector] and appealed to the directors of the station for their support. They brought with them a resolution embodying their demands on the government:

1. Payment of wages in accordance with the old norms on the next payday.
2. Immediate reduction of the cost of living.
3. Free and secret elections.
4. No punitive measures against strikers and strike spokesmen.

In the evening RIAS reported the events of the day and a little later broadcast a proclamation by Jakob Kaiser, the West German Minister for All-German Affairs, in which he declared:

> The demonstrations of the East Berlin population can come as a surprise to no one who is familiar with the intolerable conditions in the Soviet zone. Nevertheless I appeal to every East Berliner and every inhabitant of the Soviet zone to let neither sufferings nor provocations drive him into rash action. Do not endanger yourself or your fellow citizens. Only the re-estab-

[4] Arnulf Baring, *Der 17. Juni 1953*. Köln/Berlin 1957, pp. 58-62.

lishment of German unity and freedom can bring about a fundamental change in your existence.[5]

In the following days RIAS broadcast a number of reports on the events in the eastern sector of the city. Above all, Ernst Scharnowski, chairman of the Berlin section of the German Trade Union League, issued a proclamation which was broadcast at 5:30 in the morning of June 17 and heard throughout East Berlin:

> The measures that you Berlin construction workers have decided entirely on your own responsibility and without outside interference fill us with admiration and satisfaction. On the strength of the basic human rights incorporated in the constitution of the Soviet occupation zone, you are wholly justified in making these demands. Your own government formulated this declaration of rights and thereby gave you freedom to fight for better working conditions.
>
> The entire population of East Berlin can therefore put its confidence in the strongest and most successful sections of the East Berlin labor movement. Do not leave them to their own resources. They are all fighting not only for the social rights of the working class but also for the universal human rights of the entire population of East Berlin and the East Zone. Therefore support the movement of the East Berlin construction workers, municipal transportation workers, and railroad workers. All man your stations on Strausbergerplatz. The larger the participation, the more powerfully and disciplined will the movement develop and bring you success.[6]

On the morning of June 17, nearly all the larger factories and shops of East Berlin were on strike. Many thousands of workers formed marching columns, which increased in numbers as they advanced. Streetcar traffic was halted, motormen and conductors abandoned their cars and joined the demonstrators. The Stadtbahn (Elevated) ran only intermittently.

At about 7:45 the first of the giant columns of marchers left

[5] "Der Aufstand der Arbeiterschaft im Ostsektor von Berlin und in der sowietischen Besatzungszone Deutschlands," *Tätigkeitsbericht der Hauptabteilung Politik des Rundfunks im amerikanischen Sektor in der Zeit vom 16. Juni bis zum 23. Juni 1953*, p. 5.
[6] *Ibid.*, p. 8.

Strausbergerplatz, heading for Alexanderplatz and Leipziger Strasse. Heavy rain was falling. . . . When at about 8:30 the first great column of marchers turned into Leipziger Strasse from Friedrichstrasse, filling the whole width of the street, truckloads of Vopos [People's Police] arrived and cordoned off the area in front of the Ministry. The cordon was immediately reinforced by the garrisoned Vopos coming out of the building. . . . The marchers reached the police lines, and suddenly a few civilians in the front ranks slipped through. They spoke with the police officers and pointed out a few of the demonstrators. The police flung themselves on these workers, struck them and arrested them in the confusion. . . . Shortly before 9 o'clock the first Russian vehicles were to be seen in the streets of the eastern sector. Five armored reconnaissance cars curved through the crowd on Alexanderplatz; the demonstrators dodged and no one was hurt. A little later eight armored reconnaissance cars appeared in the government quarter.

In all the main streets of East Berlin, speaking choruses were heard: "Ulbricht, Pieck, and Grotewohl, we have got our belly full." . . . "We demand free elections." "We're not bums, we don't need guns." "We refuse to be slaves." "Down with Billygoat!" . . .

New columns came marching down Stalin-Allee in the direction of Alexanderplatz. One column of five thousand workers carried a placard saying: "We demand free and secret elections in all Berlin and all Germany." At an interval of five hundred yards came another column of at least twenty thousand, carrying a number of black, red, and gold flags, decorated with large bunches of flowers. Speaking choruses demanded a united free Berlin and a united free Germany.[7]

On Wednesday, June 17, the uprising reached its climax; in almost all the larger cities of East Germany and in many small towns and villages there were sympathy strikes and demonstrations. In some cities the demonstrators stormed the prisons and released the prisoners. Elsewhere they occupied town halls and Security Police headquarters and threw the files out the window. In the Halle-Bitterfeld region a strike

[7] Joachim Leithäuser, *Der Aufstand im Juni.* A documentary report. Berlin 1954, pp. 24-27.

committee was set up. It drew up a program and tried to set up an organization. But before much progress could be made, the Soviet military authorities interfered with the uprising and finally it collapsed.

On the night of June 16th detachments of the Soviet divisions stationed in the East Zone and the East German garrisoned Vopos had been directed toward the larger cities, especially Berlin. On the morning of the 17th armored reconnaissance cars dashed about among the demonstrators, and at noon tanks made their appearance. Their turrets were open. But at 1 o'clock a state of emergency was declared in large parts of the country. Now the situation became more serious. The soldiers had orders to fire; there were dead and wounded.

The Soviet commandant of Berlin issued a proclamation:

> For restoration of public order in the Soviet Sector of Berlin, the following measures are promulgated:
>
> 1. As of 1 P.M., June 17, 1953, a state of emergency is declared in the Soviet Sector of Berlin.
> 2. All demonstrations, meetings, and other assemblies of more than three persons are prohibited on streets and squares and in public buildings.
> 3. The circulation of pedestrians, motor vehicles, and other vehicles is prohibited between 9 P.M. and 5 A.M.
>
> Offenders against this order will be punished in accordance with military law.
>
> Military Commandant of the Soviet Sector of Greater Berlin.
> (signed) Dibrova, brigadier-general.

All afternoon the demonstrators made every effort not to let the tanks force them off the streets. And while groups chased back and forth, an incident of special interest occurred at the Brandenburg Arch: two workers took down the red flag that had been waving there since 1948 and replaced it for a time with a flag bearing the Berlin bear emblem. One of these workers related:

> We lay down on the western ledge and crept up slowly.

> Somebody called from below: "Watch out. They've put up a machine gun on the Hotel Adlon." The red flag was made of stiff linen; it took us almost half a minute to cut it through. Horst X. took the flag and walked erect—he doesn't get dizzy—to the ledge on the sheltered west side. Then he dropped the flag. A storm of applause broke out, the people were beside themselves. A thrill of joy ran through me.[8]

Fire was put to the flag on the ground, but it was too drenched with rain to burn. Thereupon it was torn into small bits.

But the declaration of a state of emergency made it impossible to continue the demonstrations. The demonstrators—especially in East Berlin—put up stubborn resistance. They ripped up cobblestones and threw them at the tanks, jammed crowbars into the treads, plugged up the exhaust pipes, broke off the aerials. But the unequal struggle did not last long. There were dead and wounded. Thousands were arrested.

Though large sections of the working class, numerous white-collar workers, housewives, and even members of the People's Police demonstrated on June 16 and 17 against the increased norms, the division of Berlin and Germany, the food situation, and the political pressure of the Socialist Unity Party, conspicuously few of the members of the so-called intelligentsia had participated. "Compared to the workers, the so-called intelligentsia played a meager role," writes one author. "Even where the intelligentsia actively participated in the leadership, it was only in co-operation with the workers who were dominant. . . ."[9]

Yet despite this reserve during the uprising, one cannot but be surprised that after it had failed, many intellectuals felt impelled to express their solidarity with the Party and the government. The faculties of various universities, the staffs of several theaters and many other organizations signed declarations of submission to the Party. The poet and playwright Bertolt Brecht, director of the Berliner Ensemble and

[8] Joachim Leithäuser, op. cit., p. 30.

[9] Werner Zimmermann, *Die Träger des Widerstandes.* SBZ-Archiv, Vol. 20, p. 309.

of the East Berlin Theater am Schiffbauerdamm, addressed a letter to the President of the State Council (Ulbricht), to the Soviet High Commissioner in Germany (Semyonov), and to the Premier of the German Democratic Republic (Grotewohl). Its final paragraph runs:

> History will respect the revolutionary impatience of the Socialist Unity Party of Germany. The great debate with the masses about the rhythm of socialist construction will help to sift and secure our socialist achievements. At this moment I feel the need of expressing my solidarity with the Socialist Unity Party of Germany.
>
> Yours,
>
> Bertolt Brecht[10]

Only this last paragraph of the letter was printed in the East German newspaper *Neues Deutschland*. The complete text was not published until 1965.

[10] *Theater heute,* January 1965, p. 12, and February 1965, p. 50.

Books by Günter Grass
available in paperbound editions
from Harcourt Brace Jovanovich, Inc.

Four Plays: Flood; Mister, Mister; Only Ten Minutes to Buffalo; The Wicked Cooks (HB 138)

Max: A Play (HB 221)

The Plebeians Rehearse the Uprising (HB 115)

Speak Out! Speeches, Open Letters, Commentaries (HB 160)